RELIGIOUS FREEDOM:
1965 AND 1975

WOODSTOCK STUDIES

Occasional Papers
from the
Woodstock Theological Center

VOLUME 1

The Woodstock Theological Center is an institute established in Washington, D.C., in 1974 by the Maryland and New York Provinces of the Society of Jesus, in response to the call of the Jesuit Superior General Pedro Arrupe for theological reflection on the human problems of today.

An independent institute, the Woodstock Theological Center works in collaboration with university faculties and other groups in Washington and elsewhere. These relationships afford the Center an interdisciplinary milieu for its research, seminars, symposia, and publications on such problems as ethics and nuclear power, freedom and interdependence, faith and justice, Christianity and international justice, the Church as a free society, etc.

RELIGIOUS FREEDOM: 1965 AND 1975

*A Symposium
on a
Historic Document*

Edited by

**Walter J. Burghardt, S.J.
Woodstock Theological Center**

WOODSTOCK STUDIES 1
1976

PAULIST PRESS
New York, N.Y./Ramsey, N.J.

Library of Congress
Catalog Card Number: 76-45938

ISBN: 0-8091-1993-5 (Paper)

Published by Paulist Press
Editorial Office: 1865 Broadway, N.Y., N.Y. 10023
Business Office: 545 Island Road, Ramsey, N.J. 07446

Printed and bound in the
United States of America

Contents

Introduction

George G. Higgins 1

Ecumenism and Vatican II's Declaration on Religious Freedom

Pietro Pavan 7

Dignitatis Humanae: The Unfinished Agenda

James S. Rausch 39

Critical Reflections

George Lindbeck 52

Manfred H. Vogel 54

Walter J. Burghardt, S.J. 69

Brief Biographies

Pietro Pavan 73

James S. Rausch 73

George Lindbeck 74

Manfred Vogel 74

Walter J. Burghardt, S.J. 74

Introduction

George G. Higgins

It was altogether appropriate that the American observance of the tenth anniversary of the Second Vatican Council's
Declaration on Religious Freedom should have memorialized
the late John Courtney Murray, S.J., should have been sponsored by the Woodstock Theological Center in cooperation with
the National Conference of Catholic Bishops, and should have
had as its keynote speaker Monsignor Pietro Pavan of Rome,
Father Murray's closest collaborator during the Council and
one of his most intimate personal friends. To trace in detail the
relationship between Murray, Woodstock, the American hierarchy, and Pietro Pavan insofar as the Declaration on Religious
Freedom is concerned is beyond the scope of this brief Introduction. Let me settle, then, for a few random observations and
recollections, starting with the role of the American bishops in
the area of religious freedom.

The Declaration on Religious Freedom, which had to over-
come a number of discouraging obstacles during the four years
of the Council and at times seemed in danger of being per-
manently shelved, was frequently characterized by the press as
the Council's "American" schema. That was an accurate
characterization—up to a point. The American bishops, from
the very outset of Vatican II, were almost unanimously of the
opinion that the Council simply had to come out with a forth-
right declaration on religious freedom—or, to put it negatively,
that it would be disastrous for the Council to avoid the issue or
to talk around it in vague generalities. Their energetic support
of the Declaration when at times it seemed to be in serious
jeopardy is a matter of record and will undoubtedly be singled

1

out by historians as their greatest contribution to the overall success of the Council.

On the other hand, it would be a mistake to think that the Americans won the nerve-wracking battle for religious freedom singlehandedly. The fact is that, from the outset of the Council, the majority of the fathers were in favor of a strong declaration on this crucial issue. To be sure, the document picked up added support as time went on and certain real or apparent ambiguities in the successive drafts of the working texts were clarified. Nevertheless, I dare say that even if the final vote had been taken back in 1962 instead of 1965, the Declaration would have carried. It was providential, however, that the vote was postponed until the final session of the Council, for on a matter of such far-reaching importance it was essential to have the widest possible consensus.

Though it is true, then, that the Americans from the very beginning had many allies on the issue of religious freedom and in the end had the enthusiastic support of the overwhelming majority of the fathers, the fact remains that the bishops of the United States did take the lead in pushing for the adoption of the Declaration. The record is very clear on this point.

The record will also show, of course, that it was John Courtney Murray who not only prepared the way for the Declaration by his brilliant rethinking of the development of Catholic doctrine on religious freedom, but also, in the short run, distinguished himself as one of the master draftsmen of the final Declaration.

For present purposes, it should also be noted that Murray's relationship with the American bishops during the Council was extremely cordial and that his scholarly input to their own deliberations on the matter of religious freedom was of crucial importance. He was invited to brief the entire American hierarchy on the Declaration. Moreover, when the inside story of the Council is finally written, the record will show that he drafted many, if not most, of the major interventions made by the leading members of the American hierarchy in support of the Declaration (and certainly they were among the best and most effective of all the interventions on this subject) and was consulted on the drafting of several others.

In addition, whenever the Declaration came up for discussion at the U.S. Bishops' Press Panel, it was Father Murray who was called upon to brief the media on its contents. And when at last the Declaration was adopted, many—I would say the majority by far—of the American bishops gratefully acknowledged that Murray deserved the lion's share of the credit and, to my personal knowledge, went out of their way to congratulate him very sincerely. In this connection, I can still vividly recall the feeling of satisfaction expressed by members of the hierarchy when Murray was invited by the Holy Father to concelebrate with him and a number of other bishops and *periti* on the day the Declaration was promulgated.

It was for this reason, among others, that I suggested above that it was most appropriate that the American observance of the tenth anniversary of the Declaration should have honored Father Murray's memory and should have been jointly sponsored by his beloved Woodstock and the National Conference of Catholic Bishops.

This is not to say, of course, that Murray, as an American, had no allies at the Council among the *periti* of other nations, nor is it to say that he had anything like complete control over the precise wording of the final text of the document. First and foremost, he had the unwavering support and absolutely indispensable cooperation of Monsignor Pavan, whose own theological writings, like those of Murray, had significantly helped to prepare the way for the Declaration. A distinguished theologian in his own right, Pavan was a tower of strength to Murray. As the one who first introduced them to each other at the old Woodstock College in rural Maryland several years before the Council was convened, and as one also privileged to observe them at close range as they collaborated on the Declaration during the Council, I can attest to the fact that theirs was indeed a beautiful friendship. It was a friendship based on a profound respect for each other's remarkably similar qualities of mind and heart, their common (in another sense, uncommon) respect for the dignity of man and the integrity of the human conscience, and their mutual dedication to the truth that makes men free. Again, then, it was most appropriate that Pavan should have been invited to deliver the principal address at the

American observance of the tenth anniversary of the Declaration. Murray would have applauded his selection for this assignment and undoubtedly would have agreed with every word in Pavan's masterful address.

In conclusion, let me refer again to the fact that the American bishops and a leading American theologian made a decisive —perhaps the decisive—contribution at Vatican II to the cause of religious freedom. The reason for this is not far to seek. Given the history of the United States and, more specifically, our experience in the area of religious freedom, it was to be expected that the American bishops, with the indispensable assistance of a Murray, would take the lead on this issue in the Council. Indeed they would have disgraced themselves before the world if they had failed to do so, and furthermore would have looked like pygmies in comparison with their distinguished forerunner, the late James Cardinal Gibbons of Baltimore, who almost a century ago, speaking in the city of Rome itself, publicly proclaimed the American bishops' enthusiastic commitment to the cause of religious freedom.

Cardinal Gibbons, in taking possession of his titular church in 1887, the fourth-century Basilica of S. Maria in Trastevere, did not discuss the principle of religious freedom, as such, from the point of view of Catholic doctrine. He spoke instead—with the simple but forceful eloquence for which he was noted— about the practice of religious freedom as he knew it then in the United States. "For myself," he said, "as a citizen of the United States, without closing my eyes to our defects as a nation, I proclaim, with a deep sense of pride and gratitude, and in this great capitol of Christendom, that I belong to a country where the civil government holds over us the aegis of its protection without interfering in the legitimate exercise of our sublime mission as ministers of the Gospel of Jesus Christ." For the great progress which the Church in the United States has made "under God and the fostering care of the Holy See, we are indebted in no small degree," he added, "to the civil liberty we enjoy in our enlightened republic."

In 1887, when Gibbons made this statement, there were only seventy-five bishops in the United States. In 1962, when

Vatican II was convened, there were approximately 250. Speaking, as Gibbons had done in his day, from experience, they were in a favorable position to convince those of their confreres from other lands who might have needed to be convinced that the principle of religious freedom, which derives from the essential dignity of the human person, can be and has been made to work successfully in practice, to the benefit not only of religion but of civil society as well. Perhaps no other group of bishops in the Council could have made this point as persuasively as the Americans.

And perhaps no other hierarchy is in a better position to make sure that the Declaration on Religious Freedom is accurately interpreted as time goes on. Monsignor Pavan's paper, published herewith under the auspices of the Woodstock Center, will be extremely helpful to them in this regard. With consummate tact but also with great forcefulness, Pavan repeatedly emphasized in his paper that the Declaration means precisely what it says—and nothing else. He also warned against an ominous tendency in some circles to demythologize the document, so to speak, and to negate or becloud its basic premises and conclusions. This was a very timely warning even here in the United States, where at least one theologian, in a recent analysis of the Declaration, has placed unwarranted restrictions on its meaning and its scope. This theologian talks about religious freedom almost exclusively in terms of the rights and privileges of the Church, whereas the Council's Declaration discussed it primarily as a fundamental human right (of all people everywhere) which "has its foundation in the very dignity of the human person, as this dignity is known through the revealed Word of God and by reason itself. This right of the human person to religious freedom is to be recognized in the constitutional law whereby society is governed. Thus it is to become a civil right" (no. 2).

Murray spent a lifetime developing and refining this argument in his own theological writings. In cooperation with Pavan, he helped to get it incorporated in the Council's Declaration. The fact that the authentic meaning of the Declaration is now being distorted in some ecclesiastical and theological circles is cause for discouragement; but the fact that Pavan has set the record straight, with such magisterial eloquence and authority, is cause for rejoicing. The Catholic community in the United States owes the Woodstock Theological Center (which grew out of the old Woodstock College in Maryland, where Murray lived and worked for many years) a sincere debt of gratitude for making Pavan's paper available together with an expanded version of the panel discussion which followed its presentation. I can think of no better way for John Courtney Murray's beloved Woodstock to have honored his memory.

We are also grateful to the Woodstock Center for having published Bishop Rausch's paper as a companion piece to Pavan's keynote address. The Bishop's paper is an important contribution in its own right, but it takes on added significance at this stage as an encouraging indication that the relationship between bishops and theologians in the United States—thanks in large measure to Rausch's personal leadership—is increasingly becoming one of mutual confidence and respect. This, too, can serve to remind us of our indebtedness to Father Murray; for surely no American theologian of his generation did more to prepare the way for this encouraging state of affairs.

Ecumenism and Vatican II's Declaration on Religious Freedom

Pietro Pavan

It is well known that the theme of religious freedom was treated at length during the preparatory phase of the Second Vatican Council, through the efforts of the Secretariat for Promoting Christian Unity. In this work, Emile Joseph De Smedt, Bishop of Bruges, played a leading part.

The Central Preparatory Commission of the Council met for the seventh and last time from June 12-20, 1962. Before it lay two schemata on religious freedom: one presented by Cardinal Augustin Bea as president of the Secretariat for Promoting Christian Unity, the other by the Theological Commission. The basic principles of the two documents differed substantially. The starting point of the Secretariat's text was the *dignity of the person*, seen from a moral point of view, namely, as grounded in the uprightness and integrity of conscience; the Theological Commission's starting point was constituted by the *rights of truth*. In the June 12-20 sessions there was long and lively discussion of the two texts. One group of cardinals and bishops favored the Theological Commission's document, both for theological reasons and because they held it to be fully in harmony with papal teaching, especially that of Leo XIII. But a considerable number of other cardinals and bishops favored the Secretariat's text, though they had certain reservations and proposed some changes and additions. Their reasons for supporting the text were mainly pastoral; yet there were those who also insisted that the text was sound and unassailable from a doctrinal viewpoint.

In the course of the discussion many had proposed that the

two texts should be fused into one which would harmoniously blend the two lines of theological thinking, the doctrinal and the pastoral; but a rapprochement between the two groups proved impossible. Subsequently the Theological Commission reworked its text in a shorter form, but without altering the direction of its doctrine. This second text was published in the volume *Elementa constitutionum et decretorum de quibus disceptabitur in Concilii sessionibus: Series secunda, De ecclesia et De beata Maria virgine*. It forms chapter 9 of the schema for the Dogmatic Constitution on the Church. But later the schema on the Church was reshaped and the subject of Church-state relations was omitted. In consequence, the question of religious freedom was also omitted, since this was directly connected with the theme of Church and state.

DOCUMENT OF THE SECRETARIAT FOR UNITY

During the preparatory phase of the Council the Secretariat for Promoting Christian Unity did not publish any text on religious freedom. In part, this was due to the fact that a dispute had arisen about the competence of the Secretariat to present to the Council texts that had a theological content. However, on October 22, 1962, John XXIII put the Secretariat on the same level as the other conciliar commissions and authorized it to put before the Council drafts and schemata which it judged useful for its purposes.

As a result of the Pope's decision, the Secretariat went quickly to work. In its plenary meeting held February 16-18, 1963, it decided to work out a new text on religious freedom, and this was eventually published in a separate fascicle as chapter 5 of the schema on ecumenism. It was distributed to the Council fathers on November 19, 1963, during the Second Session. (By this time Paul VI was Pope, having been elected on June 21 of the same year.) On that same morning, November 19, Bishop De Smedt presented the text in the Council, with a long and weighty *relatio* in which he set out the many reasons that made it evident that the time had come for the Catholic Church, through the mouth of the Council, to let the world know clearly her doctrinal position about religious freedom.

One of the reasons he expounded was ecumenical: if the Council did not speak out unequivocally on this issue, it might well be impossible for the ecumenical movement to develop in breadth and depth.

There are many non-Catholics, Bishop De Smedt said in his *relatio*, who feel an aversion to the Catholic Church and suspect her of Machiavellianism: she insists on religious freedom for herself in those states where Catholics are in a minority, but denies it to non-Catholics in those countries where Catholics are in the majority. De Smedt finished his *relatio* with these words:

> Our document will be considered for what it is. It is not a treatise but a pastoral decree directed to the people of our time. The whole world is waiting for this decree. In the universities, in national and international organizations, in Christian and non-Christian communities, in the press and in public opinion at large, the Church's utterance on religious freedom is being awaited, urgently awaited. It will not be impossible, we do hope, to complete our treatment of this very short but gravely important decree and approve it before the end of this second session. To your efforts, venerable fathers, we shall join ours. Our Secretariat will examine your amendments with the closest attention and the greatest speed. We shall work day and night.

During the general discussion of the Decree on Ecumenism which took place November 19-21, some fathers spoke on chapter 5, that is, on religious freedom. But on November 21 it was decided to put off the particular handling of that chapter until the following session. As a result, no vote was taken on that chapter during the Second Session. As a matter of fact, two years had to pass before any vote was taken, so complex, so heated, so tense and dramatic was the debate on this subject among the fathers and the *periti*, in the Council hall and outside.

THIRD SCHEMA

The first draft on religious freedom made up, as we have seen, chapter 5 of the schema on ecumenism. The second version appeared as an appendix to the schema labeled "Declaration No. 1," Declaration No. 2 being that on Jews and non-Christians, also in the appendix. The title of the second version was "On Religious Freedom," and its subtitle "On the Right of Person and Community to Freedom in Religious Matters." There was no vote on this second draft either. It was discussed in the Council from September 23-25. There were forty-three speeches, four of them made in the name of more than seventy fathers. Afterwards about a hundred observations and proposed amendments were sent to the Secretariat for Promoting Christian Unity.

The third schema appears as a separate document, but with the same title and subtitle as the second. It was widely thought among the fathers that the right thing would be for the Council to pronounce on religious freedom in a document distinct from the Decree on Ecumenism. Even if effective advancement of the ecumenical movement did presuppose indispensably a proclamation of the right to freedom in religious matters, the latter was nevertheless of such value in itself and of such broad application that it called for treatment in a separate document. The third schema was drafted taking account above all of the speeches made in the debate on the second schema, but also bearing in mind the observations and emendations later proposed to the Secretariat. The text appears in a thoroughly new form, which it retained substantially henceforward. In the drafting of this text as well as in subsequent redraftings down to the time when the Declaration *Dignitatis humanae* took its final shape, an outstanding part was played by John Courtney Murray, S.J. He was distinguished at all times for his unique grasp of the subject, for his wisdom, his nobility of mind, his loyalty to the Church, and his love of truth. At this point, a short digression.

The fascicle containing the third schema was distributed to the fathers on November 17, 1964; on the same day the Secretary General announced that a vote on it would be taken on November 19, under the conditions usual in the Council. In the meantime, however, a considerable number of fathers asked that the vote be put off, in accordance with article 30, par. 2, of the Council's Procedural Regulations, so as to give adequate time for a close scrutiny of the new text. The subject matter, these fathers pointed out, was of the highest importance. Besides, the new text showed substantial changes when compared with the preceding one.

The Council of Presidency accepted the plea of these fathers, and its decision was conveyed to the whole Council in a communiqué read by Cardinal Tisserant at the 126th General Congregation on November 19. There was an immediate and lively reaction from many fathers in the Council hall. The same day a petition was presented to the Pope, expressed in rather vigorous terms and carrying 441 signatures. In the same 126th Congregation, Bishop De Smedt read the *relatio* presenting the third schema. He made no change in the text. However, as he began his speech, he put a *non* before the verb *praesentamus*: "Textus quem hodie vestris suffragationibus *non* praesentamus. . . ." His reading was repeatedly interrupted by applause and at the end he received a prolonged ovation.

In this overheated atmosphere the Pope ordered the matter to be examined by the Administrative Tribunal, which had been set up inside the Council to decide questions of this kind. The Tribunal confirmed the Council of Presidency's decision, and the Pope supported the Tribunal, giving his reasons for doing so in a declaration read in his name by Cardinal Tisserant in the Council hall on November 20:

> Let the fathers know that the delay in voting was granted by the Council of Presidency because it had to be granted to conform to the Council's own regulative Ordo. Moreover, the delay was required out of respect for the freedom of the Council fathers, who are very much concerned to ponder so significant a schema with the care and at the depth it demands. As a result, the schema of the Declaration on Religious Freedom will be taken up in the next session—and, if at all possible, before any other schemata.

Thus this stormy affair ended without any Council vote even on the third schema.

Taking account of the fathers' observations on that schema and of the Theological Commission's views, the Secretariat for

Promoting Christian Unity proceeded to draft a fourth text on the right to freedom in religious matters. On May 11, 1965, the Coordinating Commission of the Council decided that this text should be sent to the fathers, together with the *relatio* with which it was being presented.

In spite of some notable changes in form and some emendations of the content, the new text reasserted the main line of argument of its predecessor. The essential elements were repeated but in a briefer, clearer, more orderly fashion. The logical thread binding them together runs more smoothly and is more easily perceived. For this reason, some saw the hand of Providence in the fact that the third schema was neither discussed in the Council hall nor voted on. This allowed a complex, delicate, sensitive theme to be more carefully worked out and presented in a form more appropriate to a document bearing the title of "Declaration."

Subsequently, in the Fourth (final) Session, we had two further redactions of the text; but in these the emendations had to do with form rather than content. In any event, they were intended only and always as minor improvements to a document already definitive in content and structure.

AMERICAN EPISCOPATE AND LINE OF ARGUMENT

I took part in the Second Vatican Council from beginning to end. At the preparatory stage I was a member of two pontifical commissions, the Theological Commission and the Commission on the Lay Apostolate. In the four sessions from the opening day, October 11, 1962, to the closing day, December 8, 1965, I was a *peritus*. I am therefore in a position to say with full assurance that the impact of the American episcopate— above all, all the bishops of the United States—was decisive (1) in bringing about the Declaration on Religious Freedom and (2) in ensuring that its main line of argument should be the one which it now exhibits.

The document comprises fifteen articles, of which the most important is no 2, which proclaims the right to freedom in religious matters and states what are the essential or constitutive elements of this right.

(1) It is a right which belongs to *all* human beings: Catholics and non-Catholics, Christians and non-Christians, believers and unbelievers or atheists. "This Vatican Synod declares that the human person has a right to religious freedom." The affirmation is simple and solemn in the extreme. It lends the document historic value, not only for the life of the Church, but, reflexively at least, for the life of the whole human family. The right to religious freedom is also such that all are bound to recognize and respect it: individuals, groups, authorities civil and religious: "all men are to be immune from coercion on the part of individuals or of social groups and of any human power. . . ."

(2) With regard to object and content, the right to religious freedom grants "immunity from coercion" understood in a double sense: "This freedom means that all men are to be immune from coercion . . . in such wise that in matters religious no one is to be forced to act in a manner contrary to his own beliefs. Nor is anyone to be restrained from acting in accordance with his own beliefs, whether privately or publicly, whether alone or in association with others, within due limits."

(3) The foundation of the right to religious freedom is the dignity of the human person ontologically understood and as known by the light of reason and through revelation. "The Synod further declares that the right to religious freedom has its foundation in the very dignity of the human person, as this dignity is known through the revealed Word of God and by reason itself."

(4) As to its nature, the right to religious freedom is such that it exists not because the state confers it but because it emerges from a person's very own dignity. In classical terms, it would be called a "natural," not a "positive," right. Nonetheless, the state is bound to reaffirm it as a civil right. "This right of the human person to religious freedom is to be recognized in the constitutional law whereby society is governed."

If we consider that right carefully in all its essential elements, we are obliged to conclude that it represents a new position in the tradition of the Catholic Church, but a new position that reveals itself as an intrinsic development in the sociopoli-

tical teaching of the Catholic Church. It is a new step forward
in that teaching, but a step forward that is not reversible—for
two reasons: (1) It is a right not entirely linked with the historical situation—even though it was because of the historical situation that the conciliar fathers decided to examine it and to take
a clear position on it. (2) It is a right founded in the dignity of
the human person—a facet of the issue I shall take up shortly.

John Courtney Murray, S.J., more than any other, put in
evidence the continuity in the teaching of the Catholic Church
in this matter.

A PERSONAL REMINISCENCE

On March 2, 1953, Cardinal Alfredo Ottaviani gave a
speech on religious freedom at the Pontifical Lateran University
(at that time still called an *athenaeum*). The speech attracted
wide attention. The following year I came to the United States
and had occasion to discuss reactions to the speech with many
people, some holding high positions of responsibility in the
Church. When I got back to Rome, I was asked by the Secretariat of State to send them a note on the subject. Rereading
that note after twenty-one years, I came across this passage,
which I had already jotted down following my first discussion
with John Courtney Murray at Woodstock College in Maryland:

> Cardinal Ottaviani seems to start from the as-
> sumption that the present Pope—Pius XII—has re-
> peated as it stands the sociopolitical teaching of Leo
> XIII. But this is neither logically necessary nor histor-
> ically factual. Christian sociopolitical teaching is not a
> closed system; it is, as the saying goes, an open sys-
> tem; and there is nothing against the idea that the
> supreme magisterium of the Church may and does ex-
> pand it with fresh additions more or less occasioned by
> historical developments. Between repetition and con-
> tradiction *datur tertium*, there is a third possibility:
> unfolding from within. What our Lord said of the
> kingdom of heaven can be said analogically of Chris-
> tian sociopolitical doctrine: it is like a seed which be-
> comes a tree. To be sure, the trunk, the branches, the
> leaves, the flowers, the fruit have an intrinsic vital

relation to the seed; but no one would dream of identifying them with the seed. Leo XIII and Pius XII contributed vigorously to the unfolding of Christian sociopolitical doctrine. If a comparison be in order, it might be said that Leo XIII's social teaching rather dealt with God in relation to man, while the present Pope, meeting a different historical situation, has dealt more with man in relation to God. The result has been new and remarkable developments.

An echo of this passage may be found in the last sentence of the first article of the Declaration: "in taking up the matter of religious freedom this sacred Synod intends to develop the doctrine of recent Popes on the inviolable rights of the human person and on the constitutional order of society."

FOUNDATION OF THE RIGHT

The universality of the right to freedom in religious matters emerges also from its foundation: the dignity of the human person, but dignity understood "ontologically." What does "ontologically" mean? It means that the document is concerned not with the *moral* dignity that belongs to a person because of the uprightness of his or her conscience, but with the very *nature* of person. This dignity is grounded on the human reality which a person is, that is, on elements rooted in his or her being as endowed with intelligence and freedom. It is a dignity that every human person possesses always and everywhere simply by being a person, and not by behaving rightly in the moral field. It is the dignity that flows from the being of the person and inheres in the being of the person and does not depend on the deeds of the person—whether these be right or wrong, whether these be right because they correspond to objective truth, or right because of invincible ignorance.

In the conciliar document three elements are explicitly considered that constitute the dignity, ontologically understood, of the human person: (1) the inescapable responsibility of every person to fix his or her own relationship with God, (2) the nature and immediacy of the relationship between person and truth, and (3) identity—or the need for a person to be himself or herself.

A RESPONSIBILITY THAT CANNOT BE RENOUNCED

One of the constituent elements of the ontological dignity, touched on by the Declaration, is the inescapable responsibility of every person to fix his or her own relationship with God—in other words, to decide his or her own eternal destiny. It is a responsibility one cannot avoid assuming, because it springs from what persons are by nature and not from what they become by their activity; hence no one can get another to replace him or her in establishing the relationship with God. "He who made you without your cooperation," says St. Augustine, "will not justify you without your cooperation. He made man without man's knowing it; He does not justify him without his willing it" (*Sermon 189*, 11-13 [*PL* 38, 823]).

Yet this responsibility cannot be exercised other than freely, and this implies the exclusion of means of coercion, especially in the domain of religion. In that domain, attitudes assumed or actions performed because we are forced have no value, no sense even, and are not accepted by God. "God calls men to serve Him in spirit and in truth. Hence they are bound in conscience but they stand under no compulsion. God has regard for the dignity of the person whom He Himself created; man is to be guided by his own judgment and he is to enjoy freedom. This truth appears at its height in Christ Jesus, in whom God perfectly manifested Himself and His ways with men" (*DH* 11).

IMMEDIACY OF RELATIONSHIP BETWEEN PERSON AND TRUTH

A second constitutive element of the dignity of the person ontologically understood is the immediacy of the relationship between person and truth, and the fact that for rightly establishing this relationship the use of coercion makes no sense and can contribute nothing; rather, it is a disturbing factor. Truth cannot be known except in the light of truth. The Council document declares: "The truth cannot impose itself except by virtue of its own truth, as it makes its entrance into the mind at once quietly and with power" (*DH* 1).

This aspect of the dignity of the person is treated at some length in paragraph 2 of the second article. It is pointed out that human beings, intelligent and free by nature and hence invested with personal responsibility for their actions, cannot fail to be aware of the need and of the duty to seek truth, especially in the domain of religion; to cleave to the truth as it gradually unfolds itself to them; to order their whole lives in the light of the truth they possess and according to its guidance; to translate truth into actions. There are three stages—to know, to love, to act—through which human beings develop and perfect themselves as persons.

As we have seen, however, truth cannot be known except in the light of truth. In the process of knowing, force from outside cannot take the place of evidence from within. Full adherence to the truth demands an act of love that can only emerge in freedom. Harmony between the truth known and life in all its expressions has no human value unless it is achieved not through pressures and impulses from without but by personal decisions. This demands, obviously, that human beings, in establishing their manifold relationship with the truth, shall be free of all coercion in social life, and the demand is rooted in the nature of the relationship itself, regardless of how each of us behaves in establishing the relationship. Hence, as the paragraph quoted says, the right to immunity from coercion persists even if it is abused; but its exercise can be hindered if the abuse amounts to subversion of public order.

It is in accordance with their dignity as persons—that is, beings endowed with reason and free will and therefore privileged to bear personal responsibility—that all men should be at once impelled by nature and also bound by moral obligation to seek the truth, especially religious truth. They are also bound to adhere to the truth, once it is known, and to order their whole lives in accord with the demands of truth.

However, men cannot discharge these obligations in a manner in keeping with their own nature unless they enjoy immunity from external coercion as well as psychological freedom. Therefore, the right to religious freedom has its foundation, not in the subjective disposition of the person, but in his very nature. In consequence, the right to this immunity continues to exist even in those who do not live up to their obligation of seeking the truth and adhering to it. Nor is the exercise of this right to be impeded, provided that the just requirements of public order are observed (*DH* 2).

IDENTITY

Personal identity, that is, being always oneself in thought, will, and action, is an objective requirement for one's dignity that is acutely recognized in our time. Thinking, willing, and acting are the three stages through which the person expresses and develops himself, i.e., his humanity, his "human being"; yet they are three stages linked by an inner relation of continuity, three stages of development. The sparks of truth which thought discloses in the mind tend to excite movements of love; and by way of these movements the sparks of truth tend to be translated, given concrete form in action. Therefore, to break this continuity in any sphere of life, but above all in the religious, by forcing a person to act in opposition to his own mind and will, or by hindering him from acting in harmony with either, is to harm deeply his dignity, to violate a fundamental right. This is the right to be always himself without hindrance in thought, in will, in action, i.e., not to be prevented from manifesting his own being through his own doing, so as to grow into what he is, namely, his humanity. Only the abuse of that right can justify public authority in suspending its exercise out of the obvious need to safeguard public order. However, the suspension of the exercise of a right does not, it is clear, imply the extinction of the right.

On his part, man perceives and acknowledges the imperatives of the divine law through the mediation of conscience. In all his activity a man is bound to follow his conscience faithfully, in order that he may come to God, for whom he was created. It follows that he is not to be forced to act in a manner contrary to his conscience. Nor, on the other hand, is he to be restrained from acting in accordance with his conscience, especially in matters religious.

For, of its very nature, the exercise of religion consists before all else in those internal, voluntary, and free acts whereby man sets the course of his life directly toward God. No merely human power can either command or prohibit acts of this kind.

However, the social nature of man itself requires that he should give external expression to his internal acts of religion; that he should participate with others in matters religious; that he should profess his religion in community. Injury, therefore, is done to the human person and to the very order established by God for human life, if the free exercise of religion is denied in society when the just requirements of public order do not so require (*DH* 3).

An Inseparable Relationship

The elements set out above which make up the content of the right to freedom in religious matters as defined and proclaimed in Vatican II should be considered simultaneously, as a whole, and should be understood in the sense given to them, as that sense *explicitly* emerges from the terms used to make it precise. These terms were chosen in the course of a minute examination and a prolonged discussion conducted with the deepest attention and with constant concern by a very great number of Council fathers. When they began to work out the document, they often found themselves holding differing or even radically contradictory positions, but as the work went on, the differences were gradually lessened and the opposition reduced, until at the last stage a convergence was reached which embraced nearly all the fathers. Because of the intimate relationship among the elements making up the document, by which they are closely linked and explain and justify one another, the document appears internally well structured and doctrinally valid only if this relationship be borne in mind. Otherwise it is impossible to grasp the interconnection among its parts and the document risks seeming unclear or even doctrinally inconsistent.

We have seen that the primary element in the right to religious freedom is the affirmation that to every human being, as a person, there belongs the right to freedom in matters religious. In this affirmation the existence and universality of the right are proclaimed with crystal clarity. But this first element ought to be viewed in relation to a second, that is, to the content or object of the right, and this is essentially negative; immunity from coercion in the twofold sense explained. For if it is maintained—as a good many fathers were led to think at the beginning—that the object of the right is a faculty, recognized and legally protected, to profess one's own religion, religious liberty ceases to be a universal right. For if a religion is not true or contains false elements, anyone who professes it thereby contributes to the spreading of error, and the spreading of error is a bad thing; therefore it cannot be the object of a right, least of all a personal right founded on personal dignity. But immunity from coercion and the exclusion of coercive means in regulating the coexistence of human beings, especially in the sensitive area of religious life, is a *universal* requirement; therefore it may be the object of a right which is itself universal.

The same must be said of the third element of the right, namely, the affirmation that it is based on the dignity of the human person. This dignity is not to be understood in the *moral* sense, as that dignity which accrues to a human person from the rightness of his conscience. A right conscience can be right and *true*, in which case it could certainly form the basis of an undoubted right. But a right conscience can also be invincibly in error and not in conformity with objective truth. In this case it represents an attitude of mind toward which there should be understanding, respect, and tolerance. In a given historical situation, such as the present one, for reasons of the common good, such conscience might be considered a reasonable and sufficient ground for the state to grant its citizens a positive right to freedom in religious matters; but it cannot constitute the solid basis of *a right of the person* such as the one proclaimed by the Declaration. A natural right, i.e., a right that is certain and universal, cannot be founded on an objective error. But in the document the dignity of the person is taken, as we have seen, in the ontological sense. It is the dignity which everybody possesses in virtue of elements that penetrate and qualify his own personal being, i.e., the inalienable responsibility to establish his relationship with God and to make decisions relative to his eternal destiny, to the immediacy of his relationship with the truth which can only be known in the light of the truth, and to his own identity, that is, his unquestionable right to be always self-identical. These elements belong certainly to every person always and everywhere. It follows that they can and in fact do constitute the objective foundation of a right which belongs to the very person and is, in the traditional terminology, "natural."

RIGHT, DUTY, LOVE

There are those who have expressed and still express disappointment about the right to religious freedom as proclaimed by the Council, on the ground that a right with a merely negative content has very little impact on religious life. It is worth saying something about this.

First, the right to religious freedom is today asserted in the constitution of nearly all civil societies (cf. P. Pavan, *Libertà religiosa e pubblici poteri* [Milan, 1965]). It is also being maintained by many that normally the right has a negative content (cf. Pio Fedele, *La libertà religiosa* [Milan, 1963]). The Catholic hierarchy assembled in Council from all parts of the world was asked the question: What does the Catholic Church think of this right? The Declaration is the answer to that question: the Catholic hierarchy declares itself in favor of the right. To dispel all misunderstanding, it fixes precisely the negative content of the right and declares it to be fundamental to the human person and hence to belong to every human being whatever his religion and even if he is an unbeliever, provided that it be understood in the sense explained in the document, that is, as essentially negative in content.

But—and here is the second point—the right does not lose its importance because of this. Precisely because it is a right with a negative content, it is based on a presupposition that reveals its very high value. The presupposition is that with this right goes the recognition that human beings as persons are entitled to a reserved area within which they are called by nature and bound by duty to act on their own initiative and responsibility. One of the major reasons why this right exists is precisely to guarantee that civil authorities recognize that this area is inviolable. This is the area in which human beings have a transcendental perspective opened up to them, the area on which Christ has shed a vivid and inextinguishable light, and where all has been seen more clearly from the moment that Christianity entered into the history of the human race.

A third and last point: religious freedom as a right exists also in function of freedom as a duty in the religious field; and in that field it tends to unfold and expand in freedom as love.

It is indeed a right that cannot fail to contribute to creating a social setting in which human beings, far from finding obstacles, are attracted toward satisfying two of their deepest exigencies which are at the same time two precise duties. The first of these concerns perhaps the most sensitive aspect of personal identity, the relation between inward belief and its outward active expressions, a relation which must be governed by sincerity. The other has to do with the relation between self and truth. This dictates that we should cleave to the truth in proportion to the degree of clarity with which it discloses itself to our minds.

Religious freedom as a right forbids the use of coercive means to force human beings to be outwardly different in religious matters from what they are within themselves, or to put pressure on them to subscribe to a religious belief to which they think they ought not subscribe. This cannot but make it easier for them to fulfil the two duties just referred to: that of professing one's religion sincerely, and that of following faithfully those rays of inner light which are, or are believed to be, true religious knowledge. That Sun which is subsistent Truth is the source from which those rays come. Here that freedom as a duty unfolds, expands, and becomes freedom as love. This love will reach its highest intensity beyond time in an immediate communion with God Himself, the highest Good, the fulness of life.

THE CHURCH AND THE RIGHT TO RELIGIOUS FREEDOM

In *Dignitatis humanae* the Church often appears as the People of God and as a divine institution hierarchically structured. Here I shall limit myself to considering three positions with regard to the Church which the fathers take up in the document.

In article 1 we read:

> First, this sacred Synod professes its belief that God Himself has made known to mankind the way in which men are to serve Him, and thus be saved in Christ and come to blessedness. We believe that this one true religion subsists in the catholic and apostolic Church, to which the Lord Jesus committed the duty of spreading it abroad among all men. Thus he spoke to the apostles: "Go, therefore, and make disciples of all nations, baptizing them in the name of the Father, and of the Son, and of the Holy Spirit, teaching them to observe all that I have commanded you" (Mt. 38:19-20). On their part, all men are bound to seek the truth, especially in what concerns God and His Church, and to embrace the truth they come to know, and to hold fast to it.

As soon as the passage quoted became known, there were unfavorable reactions. How on earth, it was said, can the Council fathers fail to see how unsuitable it is for the Church to affirm so solemnly that the Catholic religion is the only way of salvation established by God, in the very same document in which it proclaims that all human beings have the same right to freedom in religious matters?

All the same, after the first mainly emotional reactions, and after the text had been examined more calmly, the opinion spread widely that the fathers had been right, honest, and candid in inserting this passage into the document. In this way the Church proclaims the right to religious freedom without any mental reservations. It presents itself with its true credentials, as it declares itself to be *today* what it has always thought and claimed to be in the past and will in the future, namely, the institution on which its divine Founder has conferred the mandate to announce and make effective the only true message of salvation. If the Church has proclaimed the right to religious freedom, it is because it judges it to be in full harmony with that

message. "This Vatican Synod takes careful note of these de-
sires in the minds of men. It proposes to declare them to be
greatly in accord with truth and justice. To this end, it searches
into the sacred tradition and doctrine of the Church—the treasury out of which the Church continually brings forth new
things that are in harmony with the things that are old" (*DH* 1).

Article 6 deals with the protection and promotion of the
right to religious freedom and affirms that "the care of the right
to religious freedom devolves upon the people as a whole, upon
social groups, upon government, and upon the Church and
other religious communities, in virtue of the duty of all toward
the common welfare, and in the manner proper to each." With
regard to the specific task of the state, a paragraph from the
Encyclical *Pacem in terris* (no. 36) is referred to: "in our time
the common good is chiefly guaranteed when personal rights
and duties are maintained. The chief concern of civil authorities
must therefore be to ensure that these rights are acknowledged,
respected, coordinated with other rights, defended, and pro-
moted, so that in this way each one may be helped to more easily carry out his duties. For to safeguard the inviolable rights of
the human person and to facilitate the fulfilment of his duties
should be the essential office of every public authority." The
Declaration then goes on (no. 6):

> Therefore, government is to assume the safeguard of
> the religious freedom of all its citizens, in an effective
> manner, by just laws and by other appropriate means.
> Government is also to help create conditions favorable
> to the fostering of religious life, in order that the peo-
> ple may be truly enabled to exercise their religious
> rights and to fulfil their religious duties, and also in
> order that society itself may profit by the moral quali-
> ties of justice and peace which have their origin in
> men's faithfulness to God and to His holy will.

Dealing with the duties of the state regarding the right to
religious freedom, the Council confined itself to examining and
evaluating concordats as a way of settling relations of Church
and state. Three trends of thought came to the fore. The first
judged concordats favorably: they afford the Church favorable

conditions for carrying out her specific mission. The second judged them unfavorably: they often impinge rather perniciously on the life of the Church, restricting her freedom of action in such delicate matters as the selection and nomination of bishops. The third pointed out that there is no a priori solution of the problem: only historical situations, which vary greatly, can suggest or call for one solution rather than another. Hence, should it be decided to deal with the problem, only a general, hypothetical treatment would be possible.

Concordats are not treated explicitly in the Declaration, but it is arguable that, implicitly, the third of these lines is followed, with the addition that whenever one religious community—the Catholic Church, for example—is granted a special juridical position by the civil society, every care should be taken to ensure that other religious bodies, and in fact all citizens, are guaranteed the exercise of the right to religious freedom, and that the principle of juridical equality for all is not compromised by direct or indirect discrimination on religious grounds.

> If, in view of peculiar circumstances obtaining among certain peoples, special legal recognition is given in the constitutional order of society to one religious body, it is at the same time imperative that the right of all citizens and religious bodies to religious freedom should be recognized and made effective in practice.
> Finally, government is to see to it that the equality of citizens before the law, which is itself an element of the common welfare, is never violated for religious reasons whether openly or covertly. Nor is there to be discrimination among citizens (*DH* 6).

Article 13 affirms that the Church needs full liberty in carrying out her mission, and for two reasons. The first reason is her divine mandate to preach the gospel to all nations and to establish it in practice. "In human society and in the face of government, the Church claims freedom for herself in her character as a spiritual authority, established by Christ the Lord. Upon this authority there rests, by divine mandate, the duty of going out into the whole world and preaching the gospel to every creature." Secondly, "The Church also claims freedom for herself in her character as a society of men who have the right to live in society in accordance with the precepts of Christian faith." But it should be observed that if the Church puts forward these reasons for claiming religious freedom for herself, it does not follow that the freedom she demands for herself and for each of her members is different in content from the freedom she proclaims for all human beings and for all other religious communities. Rather, remembering that every right is defined by its object, it can and should be said that the freedom the Church claims as a right for herself is the same as that she requires for all others, that is, freedom as a right to immunity from coercion in the twofold sense laid down in article 2.

As far as the likely repercussions of the Declaration on the life of the Church are concerned, some fathers feared that they would be rather negative, but the majority maintained that, in the long run at least, they could only be positive, because

> where the principle of religious freedom is not only proclaimed in words or simply incorporated in law but also given sincere and practical application, there the Church succeeds in achieving a stable situation of right as well as of fact and the independence which is necessary for the fulfilment of her divine mission. This independence is precisely what the authorities of the Church have always claimed in society. At the same time, the Christian faithful, in common with all other men, possess the civil right not to be hindered in leading their lives in accordance with their conscience (*DH* 13).

Moreover, when religious freedom, in the shape of a right to immunity from coercion, is allowed to all human beings and religious communities on the grounds of personal dignity, and when that right is always and everywhere respected and safeguarded, this is likely to create in the human family as a whole the most favorable conditions to enable everybody, even in the religious field, to follow the light of truth as it breaks on the mind. In such conditions obstacles that arise from the social context and that sometimes make it difficult to follow that light would be eliminated or at least reduced. This must be an advantage for the Church, since, in the long run at least, truth always ends by dissolving error. The last sentence of the last paragraph of no. 13 reads: "Therefore, a harmony exists between the freedom of the Church and the religious freedom which is to be recognized as the right of all men and communities and sanctioned by constitutional law."

To prevent misunderstanding, a few points should be clarified. The freedom of the Church can be understood in three ways: as right, as duty, as love—or, more exactly, as the expression of love, putting love into practice. Understood as the affirmation of a right, the freedom of the Church considered in its content or object, immunity from coercion, is identical with the freedom which all human beings and communities have in religious matters. This is the freedom proclaimed in the Council document. But considered in relation to its source, the Church's freedom differs from that proper to individuals or to other communities, because the Church is convinced that her freedom belongs to her additionally, and even primarily, in virtue of her divine mandate to carry on her mission for the benefit of all mankind.

Understood as the fulfilment of a duty and as the expression of love, the Church's freedom belongs to her alone: it is the freedom which the Church exercises in carrying out her specific saving mission. But there is a close relationship between the freedom of the Church asserted as a right and the same freedom lived and expressed at the same time as duty and as love. For the recognition of, respect for, and effective safeguarding of the freedom of the Church as a right is an indispensable condition for the full performance of her mission, that is, for putting into practice, without undue obstacles, her freedom considered as fulfillment of duty and exercise of love—the love of Christ and of his mystical body.

Article 14 looks at religious freedom from another point of view, that of the *method* by which the Church carries out her mission. During the last two sessions of the Council, some fathers could not rid themselves of the fear that to proclaim this right might unfavorably affect the Church's apostolic commitment. They even thought that ill-instructed Catholics might easily take the right to imply that all religions are equal, and that therefore it is not worth while to engage in spreading Catholicism. This explains why the first paragraph of no. 14 reaffirms in solemn form a Catholic imperative: "In order to be faithful to the divine command 'Make disciples of all nations' (Mt. 28:19), the Catholic Church must work with all urgency and concern 'that the Word of God may run and be glorified' (2 Th. 3:1)." For this reason the fathers exhort all the people of God to "be about their task of spreading the light of life with all confidence and apostolic courage, even to the shedding of their blood." At the same time they remind them never to use in apostolic work methods contrary to the letter and spirit of the gospel; and coercive methods are, without a shadow of doubt, so contrary. Rather they should, as living members of the mystical body of Christ, which is the Church, share vigorously in her mission, putting all their trust in methods that befit the nature of that mission. These are: (1) understanding for others, for their personal dignity and rights, together with diligent, patient, and persevering love; (2) prayer, sacrifice, and Christian witness in living; (3) the virtue of God's word, the strength of its appeal, the action of the Holy Spirit on people's minds—an action which is never wanting, an action which unfolds in accordance with the plan of salvation but is folded in the deepest mystery, an action which makes itself known also as an invitation to enter the kingdom of Christ, to enter knowingly and freely by an act of faith which is a free response of man's love to the free appeal of God's love, each of them actuated in Christ, the divine Word made man, the Redeemer.

The disciple is bound by a grave obligation towards Christ his Master ever more adequately to understand the truth received from him, faithfully to proclaim it, and vigorously to defend it, never—be it understood—having recourse to means that are incompatible with the spirit of the gospel. At the same time, the charity of Christ urges him to act lovingly, prudently, and patiently in his dealings with those who are in error or in ignorance with regard to the faith. All is to be taken into account—the Christian duty to Christ, the life-giving Word which must be proclaimed, the rights of the human person, and the measure of grace granted by God through Christ to men,

who are invited freely to accept and profess the faith
(*DH*, no. 14).

THE CONSTITUTIONAL STATE

During the initial drafting of *Dignitatis humanae*, a
number of fathers had in mind two models of the state: the
Catholic-confessional state and the secular state. These two
models they had met, in various degrees, in their reading of history or in their experience. These fathers rightly thought that to
proclaim a universal personal right to religious freedom, and
consequently to proclaim the same right for all religious bodies,
was doctrinally incompatible with the Catholic-confessional
state. Hence they drew the conclusion that the proclamation
would imply that the Church accepted the other model they had
in mind, the secular state—a model about which the supreme
magisterium had often spoken very unfavorably. This explains
why these same fathers kept feeling reluctant to acknowledge
and proclaim the right in question. But the model on which our
document relies is neither the Catholic-confessional state nor
the secular state, but the democratic-social state founded on law
—what the American world would call the constitutional state.
This was a model which Pius XII had already regarded favorably; and John XXIII in the Encyclical *Pacem in terris* turns all
his social-political thinking toward that model, tracing out its
main features and giving a substantially favorable assessment of
it in these terms (nos. 45-46):

> In modern times, when political bodies are or-
> ganized juridically, we notice first of all the tendency
> to write in concise and limpid phraseology a charter of
> fundamental human rights, which is, as often as not,
> inserted in the state constitutions or is an integral part
> of the same.
> Secondly, there is also an inclination to determine
> juridically, by the compilation of a document called
> the "Constitution," the procedures through which the
> governing powers are to be created, along with their
> mutual relations, the spheres of their competence, the
> forms or the methods they are obliged to follow in the
> performance of their office.
> The relations between the government and the

governed are then set forth in terms of rights and
duties; and it is clearly laid down that the paramount
task assigned to government officials is that of recognizing, respecting, reconciling, protecting, and promoting the rights and duties of citizens.

It is, of course, impossible to accept the theory
which professes to find the original and single source
of civic rights and duties, of the binding force of the
Constitution, and of a government's right to command, in the mere will of human beings, individually
or collectively. However, the tendencies to which we
have referred do clearly show that the men and women
of our time have become increasingly conscious of
their dignity as human persons. This awareness, while
it prompts them to claim a share in the public ad-
ministration of their country, also accounts for the
demand that their own inalienable and inviolable
rights be protected by law. It also requires that public
authorities be constituted in conformity with constitutional norms and that they perform their specific func-
tions within the limits of law.

This explains why during the Council it was widely believed that
there was a relation of cause and effect between *Pacem in terris*
and the Declaration on Religious Freedom. Without the Encyclical the Council probably could not have formulated the Declaration as it stands. John Courtney Murray, fully realizing
that the right to religious freedom as proclaimed in the Council
document could not be harmonized with a juridical system other
than that inspired by the model of the constitutional state, devoted his attention and skill to making sure that this model
would be kept to the fore whenever problems arose about the
relations between the right to religious freedom and civil authority, or between Church and state.

Now the constitutional state takes two distinctive lines of
approach with regard to the religious beliefs of its citizens. The
first line is that the state is and regards itself as unqualified to
decide the merits and contents of religious systems. It is not its
business to judge whether a religion is true or not, or whether
there are elements of truth in it, or, if so, what they are. These
things are outside its competency. The second line is that the
constitutional state believes it has a positive duty with regard to

religion, above all with regard to the right of the citizens to religious freedom. With regard to this right, as to every other fundamental right, the civil authorities feel bound to undertake two courses of action. The first is mainly juridical, namely, to recognize, respect, safeguard, and promote that right, and to limit its exercise in those cases where its abuse may consistently compromise public order. The second is mainly political, namely, to ensure that the citizens do not lack means to exercise their religious rights and fulfil their religious duties—in other words, to live their religious life according to their own convictions.

These two lines of approach are those which the constitutional state follows with regard to all spiritual values. It is, for example, not part of the function of public authority to decide whether a scientific theory is credible or not, whether or not a philosophical system objectively discloses the deepest aspects of reality, whether a work of art is or is not genuine art. But certainly it has a duty to acknowledge, respect, safeguard, and promote the rights to personal freedom in scientific research, philosophical inquiry, and artistic creations, just as it is bound to take steps to ensure that its citizens have access to the means for research, inquiry, and the pursuit of the arts.

Accordingly, because the constitutional state is and holds itself to be unqualified to judge the merits and the content of religious beliefs, it does not follow that it should be regarded as neutral or skeptical in matters of religion, or hostile to religion and hence as openly at odds with the gospel message and with the Church's sociopolitical teachings. It is integral to the model of the constitutional state that it should have a positive policy toward religion but should carry out that policy in a way that answers to its nature. It can and should be maintained that such a policy cannot fail to benefit religion.

First of all, by effectively safeguarding the right to religious freedom the state makes it less difficult for its citizens to fulfil their religious duties. This must, in the long run, benefit the truth; for those who belong to the true religion are thus enabled to profess it and propagate it, and those who are in error have the chance to discover that true religion, but in a way that corresponds to their dignity and to the nature of the relationship between person and truth. This means, in the light of truth and not by force of improper pressures from outside—pressures that can contribute nothing to a right relationship between person and truth.

Secondly, by seeing to it that the citizens do not lack means to fulfil their religious duties, the constitutional state contributes to making that fulfillment less arduous, and so contributes also to God's being honored in a way pleasing to Him, i.e., by acts of worship done freely out of religious conviction.

Finally, by preventing abuses of religious freedom, the citizens are called upon to attend to *true* religious freedom, which is to be professed in order to raise one's mind to higher levels, and without violating the rights of others or inflicting harm on society.

UNJUSTIFIED INTERPRETATIONS

In the years since the Council, especially in very recent times, doctrinal positions on our theme which were widely held in the preconciliar Catholic tradition have emerged again. I shall mention three of them.

The first maintains that only the one who is in the truth, therefore only a Catholic, has an intrinsic or natural right to religious freedom. The one who is not in the truth, that is, a non-Catholic, if he has a right to religious freedom, has it only as a positive or legal right, conferred on him by the state for the public good. This right is being granted today by nearly all states because of the typical features that mark the modern era, but it could also lose its validity in some more or less distant future, if the historical situation were to change.

The second line being revived is that which claims a preeminent juridical position for the Church in civil societies as something demanded by theology and reason. The reason advanced is always the same: only the Church possesses the truth; it cannot, therefore, be put on the same level as other religious bodies. They may have some elements of truth, but they also have others which are false.

The third line being resurrected concerns the state. It is being maintained, on theological-moral principles, that the state cannot be anything but Catholic. The basic reason alleged is the same: as individuals are bound to pay homage to the truth, so is the state, in its own way and by means that it alone possesses. And in the religious field the truth is Catholicism.

Obviously, we cannot tackle here the many complex problems that these three lines of approach raise in theology, philosophy, and history. We must confine ourselves to a few points. The first concerns the relation between these three contentions and the Council document. It is not hard to understand that the study of these positions should be taken up again and pursued further. It is even understandable that someone might hold as a personal opinion that, on the strictly doctrinal level, only the positions described exhibit an inner coherence of their own. But to start from the assumption that the Council document is valid only to the extent that it squares with these contentions or, more surprising still, to make every effort to show that these contentions find support in the document—this is not acceptable. The document is what it is, and it can only be understood by giving its words the meaning they have in common usage and in the context of the document itself.

As for the right to religious freedom, there is no possible doubt that what is proclaimed by the Council is a right which allows of no distinctions; it is exactly the same for everybody, i.e., a universal right which belongs to every human being as a person. Hence it belongs to all the citizens of every civil society: to Catholics and non-Catholics, to Christians and non-Christians, to believers and nonbelievers. As I have explained, it is such because it is grounded on elements intrinsic to personhood, and therefore found in every human being always and everywhere. Moreover, as soon as it became known that this right had been proclaimed, it was in this sense that it was welcomed by the whole world and in all cultural environments. It was welcomed, that is to say, not as a reaffirmation by the Council of the Church's traditional, preconciliar position but as a new stance in regard to individuals, to other religious bodies, and to the civil authorities themselves. Thus every attempt to find grounds in the document for returning to preconciliar positions is useless.

A more complex problem concerns the preeminence to be

assigned to the Church in the legal systems of civil societies. It is maintained that the Church herself simply must, on theological and rational principles, claim such preeminence, since she knows herself to be the only true religion. What can be said with certainty is that in *Dignitatis humanae* nothing can be found to support the idea that this preeminence is reasserted there. The Declaration puts the emphasis exclusively on the Church's freedom to carry on her mission. The Catholic hierarchies have always claimed this freedom and do so no less forcefully today, pointing out also, and even primarily, the mandate that the Church has received from her divine Founder to preach and put into practice the gospel message of salvation.

> Among the things which concern the good of the Church and indeed the welfare of society here on earth —things therefore which are always and everywhere to be kept secure and defended against all injury—this certainly is pre-eminent, namely, that the Church should enjoy that full measure of freedom which her care for the salvation of men requires. This freedom is sacred, because the only-begotten Son endowed with it the Church which he purchased with his blood. It is so much the property of the Church that to act against it is to act against the will of God. The freedom of the Church is the fundamental principle in what concerns the relations between the Church and governments and the whole civil order (*DH* 13).

But neither here nor elsewhere in the document is there any indication that the Church claims a singular position for herself. In the same section, as we have seen, it is stated rather that, wherever religious freedom as set out in the Declaration is sanctioned by the law and sincerely put into practice, the Church's demands for freedom in the exercise of her mission are fully justified.

I have pointed out that article 6 of the document takes into account the hypothesis that one religious community might be assigned special recognition in a civil constitution. However, such special recognition is being connected to a given historical situation and not to a doctrinal exigency. This applies even if the community in question be the Catholic Church. What has been said here seems confirmed by the message which Paul VI addressed to the political authorities of the whole world at the closing of Vatican II, in which he asks only freedom for the Church.

> In your earthly and temporal city, God constructs mysteriously His spiritual and eternal city, His Church. And what does this Church ask of you after close to two thousand years of experiences of all kinds in her relations with you, the powers of the earth? What does the Church ask of you today? She tells you in one of the major documents of this Council. She asks of you nothing but freedom, the freedom to believe and to preach her faith, the freedom to love her God and to serve Him, the freedom to live and to bring to men her message of life. Do not fear her. She is made after the image of her Master, whose mysterious action does not interfere with your prerogatives but heals everything human of its fatal weakness, transfigures it, and fills it with hope, truth, and beauty.

As for the Catholic state, it is indisputable that neither *Pacem in terris* nor *Dignitatis humanae* has this state before it as a model; instead, each takes, as we have seen, the constitutional democratic-social state, a model which in modern times, especially in the West, has more and more asserted itself both in the world of thought and in legal and political reality in an increasing number of states. It is equally indisputable that in both documents the constitutional model is, by implication at least, judged as capable of being harmonized with the Catholic vision of human reality. Hence it is legitimate to argue that if there have existed Catholic states or states calling themselves Catholic, or if they come to exist, it is not because they are necessarily called for by the gospel, or because the Church's official socio-political teaching constantly maintains that, doctrinally speaking, only such states are in conformity with the gospel. If they exist or come to exist, they too are to be regarded as a product of a particular historical situation.

It should be added that if anywhere, in the future, a Catholic state or one calling itself such should be established, there too the Church would have to go on asserting and vindicating the right to religious freedom. She would also have to speak thus with reference to all the citizens of that state, Catholic and non-Catholic, Christian and non-Christian, believers and nonbelievers. The reason is obvious. The right to religious freedom as proclaimed by Vatican II is a fundamental right of the person, and fundamental personal rights belong to the content of the gospel message, which it is the Church's divinely-given mission to preach and put into practice.

In that case, someone rather scandalized might object, the Church would be standing up for the atheist's right to remain an atheist. Undoubtedly, in the sense that an atheist citizen cannot be compelled by any form of coercion to give up his atheism and profess a religion, whatever it may be. For that matter, recourse to coercion in such a case is not only the violation of a right, it is also nonsensical. The passage from atheism to religious faith cannot be the result of pressures from outside; if it is genuine, it is a profound movement of the spirit, in which two characteristic elements of spiritual life are harmoniously combined, knowledge and love. This experience cannot happen other than freely.

HOMAGE TO THE TRUTH

What has just been said might give the impression that *Dignitatis humanae* shows small esteem for the truth. The contrary is true. Truth is constantly the unifying and vitalizing principle in the Declaration—so much so that the document might be called a homage to truth. I shall limit myself to a few remarks on this.

In the first place, the document is based on truth. The dignity of the human being as a person is a truth, this dignity being understood in the ontological sense, i.e., in the constituent elements of the human person. These are (1) the inalienable responsibility of every person to establish his own relationship with God and to make decisions with regard to his eternal destiny; (2) the immediacy of the relationship between the human person and the truth, a relationship that cannot be settled except in the light of truth; (3) identity, the inward need of the person to remain always self-identical through the three stages in which he achieves from within himself his growth as a human being: thought, love, and action.

In the second place, the document calls attention to some characteristic features of the process by which truth is known. This is an intimately personal and unrepeatable process, yet one which is carried out not in isolation but in communion with others.

> Truth, however, is to be sought after in a manner proper to the dignity of the human person and his social nature. The inquiry is to be free, carried on with the aid of teaching or instruction, communication, and dialogue. In the course of these, men explain to one another the truth they have discovered, or think they have discovered, in order thus to assist one another in the quest for truth. Moreover, as the truth is discovered, it is by a personal assent that men are to adhere to it (*DH* 3).

Moreover, it is noticeable that human beings, in communicating to one another the sparks of truth which knowledge is, feel deeply and irresistibly that their dignity calls for sincerity, both in the sense that they ought to communicate the truth to others as they discover it and see it within themselves and in the sense of feeling morally obliged to embrace what they feel to be true in what is communicated to them. But sincerity is a flower that takes root and grows only in those social settings where freedom is a fundamental criterion governing interpersonal relationships.

But the Declaration also reverts frequently to the relation between human beings and objective truth, and to the fascination which truth exerts over them—above all, the living truth which is Christ the divine Word made man. "The Truth cannot impose itself except by virtue of its own truth, as it makes its entrance into the mind at once quietly and with power" (no. 1). "Not by force of blows does his rule [Christ's rule] assert its claims. Rather, it is established by witnessing to the truth and by hearing the truth, and it extends its dominion by the love whereby Christ, lifted up on the cross, draws all men to himself" (no. 11). "Therefore [the apostles] rejected all 'carnal weapons.' They followed the example of the gentleness and respectfulness of Christ. And they preached the word of God in the full confidence that there was resident in this word itself a divine power able to destroy all the forces arrayed against God and to bring men to faith in Christ and to his service" (no. 11). "Let Christians walk in wisdom in the face of those outside, 'in the Holy Spirit, in unaffected love, in the word of truth' (2 Cor. 6:6-7). Let them be about their task of spreading the light of life with all confidence and apostolic courage, even to the shedding of their blood" (no. 14).

I think, then, that we can legitimately conclude that the Second Vatican Council, proclaiming the right to religious freedom in an age like ours ridden with skepticism and materialism, an age in which totalitarian regimes and tendencies still play a large part, paid homage to truth by reconfirming its own trust in truth. If the Catholic Church in the course of her life through centuries of history has emerged from countless crises with renewed vital energy, this is not so much because of the favor and support of earthly powers which she has from time to time enjoyed, not because of the privileged legal positions which states have sometimes conferred on her, but rather, primarily if not exclusively, because of a confidence always robust and undiminished in the divine efficacy of the message of salvation of which she is the bearer.

Finally, I can say with full sincerity that all those who played a part in working out the Council document on religious freedom, from its beginning to the time when it took its final shape, were driven by one motive force: love of the truth. They had only one goal: to bear witness to the truth. Among them, there is no doubt, one man always stood out, not so much because of his physical stature but much more because of the nobility of his mind: John Courtney Murray.

Dignitatis Humanae:
The Unfinished Agenda

James S. Rausch

I am not by position or profession a scholar, but one concerned more directly with pastoral life and public policy in the Church. Consequently, I shall approach the document *Dignitatis humanae* from that perspective. Specifically, I wish to probe some of the pastoral and policy implications of the Declaration for the life of the Church in the United States today.

The theme of this essay will be twofold: first, to relate *Dignitatis humanae* to two other significant social teachings of the aggiornamento, *Gaudium et spes* and *Octogesima adveniens*; secondly, to illustrate the implications of these documents in terms of two specific cases or policy issues prominent in the American Church today. In developing this theme, I shall draw extensively on the work of the late John Courtney Murray, who collaborated so closely with Pietro Pavan in the preparation of Vatican II's Declaration on Religious Freedom.

FROM CHURCH AND STATE TO CHURCH AND SOCIETY

John Murray's writings are not only a good guide for learning how the Declaration on Religious Freedom came to be; they also provide an excellent means of measuring the significance of the text. Murray, like Pavan, labored exhaustively for three years to shape the Declaration into the finely honed piece of politico-moral analysis which we now have in *Dignitatis humanae*; yet, in the postconciliar period, Murray was noticeably modest in his assessment of the significance of the document. In a lecture given four months after the Council, Murray argued that the achievement of *Dignitatis humanae* "was simply to

bring the Church abreast of the developments that have oc-
curred in the secular world."[1]

If one reads all of Murray's commentaries, it is clear that
his intent was not to diminish the theological significance of
Dignitatis humanae but to place it in historical perspective. In
his most extended English analysis of the text,[2] Murray argued
that the specific focus of the Declaration had transformed the
traditional theology of Church and state in Catholic thought,
and had opened the way for the discussion of the broader question of *Gaudium et spes* about the role of the Church in society.
Even as he labored in the midst of the Council to shape and sal-
vage the Declaration on Religious Freedom, Murray stoutly
maintained that it is this second question, Church and society,
which is the dominant issue of our age.

The contemporary question of Church and society, however, is dependent upon the classical question of Church and state
in structure and substance. It is for this reason that *Dignitatis
humanae* and *Gaudium et spes* should be read in tandem. To
understand the structural relationship of the two texts, it is necessary to see the juridical Church-state problem as the inner
core of the broader substantive relationship of the Church and
society in its political, economic, and cultural dimensions.

The relationship between the classical and contemporary
questions is structural in the sense that the nature of the
Church-state relationship in a given political culture directly
and significantly shapes the field within which the Church can
exercise prophetic witness in society. The Church-state relationship sets at least provisional boundaries or parameters for
the style and substance of ecclesial presence in a society. The
boundaries are provisional in the sense that the Church cannot
in theory, and often will not in practice, allow its posture in society to be determined by the secular power. While denying this
possibility in principle, it is true, nonetheless, that differing
Church-state arrangements do produce observable differences in
the life of the local Church. If a systematic study of Church and
state were pursued today in Poland, Brazil, South Africa, Swit-
zerland, and England, it would be clear, I think, that the classical issue of Church-state is an essential factor in determining

how the contemporary issue of Church-society takes concrete historical shape.

In contrast to earlier formulations of the classical question, Vatican II sought to shape the Church-state relationship in the direction of according to the state a limited secular role. *Dignitatis humanae* roots the limiting principles in the political nature of the state and the theological nature of the Church.[3] The description of the state in the Declaration is cast in the constitutional mold; except for specific questions of preserving public order, the realm of religious truth, practice, and witness is placed beyond the competence and care of the state.[4]

The Church, in turn, seeks neither privilege nor special protection from the state, only the freedom to fulfil its religious mission and ministry in society. At times that mission will move it to cooperate with the state in fostering the common good; at other times the same mission will lead the Church to stand as a principal critic of the state. In either case the freedom of the Church is claimed as a right, logically linked with the right to religious freedom possessed by every person in society. The full range of personal religious freedom demands as a corollary the right of ecclesial freedom.[5] Neither is a concession by the state: they belong by nature to the person and the religious community. The way in which the Church should *exercise* her freedom is the question that opens the agenda to the contemporary issue of the Church in society.

The treatment of the classical and contemporary questions in the documents of Vatican II helps us to state the unfinished agenda of the Church in America more clearly. The concept of the limited or constitutional state espoused in *Dignitatis humanae* is complemented in *Gaudium et spes* by a style of ministry in society that is based upon the dignity of the person and works through the agency of the Church as the People of God. The vision of social ministry espoused in *Gaudium et spes* is based upon the safeguarding of human dignity, the protection of human rights, and the promotion of unity in the human family.[6] These broadly defined policy objectives arise from and are related to the Church's pastoral life. In the conciliar document there is a clear logical line drawn between the pastoral presence of the

Church in society and the policy positions the Church espouses in the social system. To protect and promote human dignity requires a definition of the pastoral task in social-structural terms.

It also requires a style of Church presence in society that uses fully the experience, life, and witness of the constituency of the Church. *Gaudium et spes* is clear that the Church's ministry is religious, not political, in nature; yet the animating religious vision of the gospel has substantial political potential.[7] The way the religious ministry properly finds political expression is through the conscientious witness of Christians fully participating in the life of their society.

Relating the Church-state and Church-society questions to an American context makes it possible to clarify a pervasive confusion which persists in the Church and in the wider society. The Church-state relationship in the United States is, of course, basically contained in the First Amendment's legal doctrine of separation. Without exploring the intricacies of jurisprudential and constitutional interpretation surrounding this clause, it is fair to say, I think, that the fundamental intent of the separation clause is to place the realm of religious truth and life beyond the reach of state power. The separation of Church and state leaves the Church free to be the Church. In this sense the First Amendment can be read as setting the Church free for social ministry.

In practice, however, the separation clause is sometimes used either in the churches or in society to argue against the legitimacy of religious witness on social issues. Separation in this sense can be used to isolate the Church from significant social ministry. Hence the need to clarify precisely what is the structural relationship of the classical and contemporary questions in the American context. To state the case with strangling brevity, the separation clause governs the specific juridical relationship between the institution of the Church and the institution of the state. This critical but limited relationship neither exhausts the role of the Church in society nor defines the relationship of the Church to those areas of society which lie beyond the limited confines of the state. Indeed, even in regard to the state, the separation clause, while rightly preventing any special privilege for the Church, cannot be used legitimately to silence or stifle Christian evaluation of the policies of the state.

The wider range of issues that fall outside the precise structural issue of Church and state constitutes the field of prophetic witness, pastoral ministry, and social policy for the Church. To use the separation clause to govern these areas would be to hinder and obstruct the ministry for justice that the Church has described as a constitutive dimension of her existence.[8]

The legitimate legal doctrine of separation of Church and state is very much in accord with Vatican II's Declaration on Religious Freedom; it allows the Church to be the Church. What must be constantly watched is any attempt in the practical or theoretical order, coming from within the Church or without, to translate the separation of Church and state into a prevailing doctrine of separating the Church from society. This approach confines the Church to the purely private or personal sphere of existence and denies it public significance.

The strongest safeguard against any such move is an educated laity shaped by the full dimensions of Christian teaching as reflected in *Dignitatis humanae* and *Gaudium et spes*. The cultivation of such a lay constituency is a task of both religious and secular significance; the two dimensions of the task are summarized in the concept of the Christian as citizen.

THE CHRISTIAN AS CITIZEN

The concept of the Christian as citizen has *roots* in the theological discussion of Church and state, it has *relevance* to the contemporary shape of society, and it provides a specific *role* for the Church in its ministry of pastoral care today.

In the postwar years, when Murray was writing extensively to demonstrate that the thesis-hypothesis formulation of the Church-state question was neither adequate nor necessary, he focused on the concept of the citizen in Catholic political thought to illustrate how Catholic teaching had developed beyond its nineteenth-century conception. In the shift from the nineteenth- to the twentieth-century statement of the Church-state question, Leo XIII stands as a pivotal figure. Murray's careful probing of the writings of Leo XIII uncovered a complex pattern of thought in which much of the tone and style reflected Leo's immediate predecessors, but some of the substantive concepts pointed to a new stage of development.[9]

The development consisted in Leo XIII's restatement of the traditional Gelasian doctrine of the spiritual and temporal power in society. In the Gelasian and medieval formulation of the question, the rationale for the cooperation of Church and state was the common good of the one "great society" in which both Church and state played distinct roles. Leo XIII recognized that the great society of medieval Christendom had passed into the pages of history. He recast the rationale of Church-state relationships in terms of the citizen whom both powers served. The person who was both Christian and citizen became the raison d'être of both institutions; they were called to a cooperative pattern of life, because both were required for the full development of the citizen.

The central role Leo XIII gave to the concept of citizenship in terms of the structure of Church-state relations was obscured by the passive conception he had of the citizen's role in society. Leo XIII's concept of government was paternalistic, not participatory. The citizen was to be served by Church and state, but neither was accountable to the person it served in any significant way. The development of an active concept of citizenship in Catholic political thought was the work of Pius XII and John XXIII. Pius XII's early pontificate was framed by the threat of totalitarian governments of the left and right. In the face of this mirror image of absolute power vested in the state, Pius XII sought to surround the citizen with a complex of rights which would both defend the citizen against unjust intrusion and allow the person to participate in shaping the political system.

In a statement that has permeated Catholic social thought, Pius XII described the person as "the subject, foundation, and end of the social order."[10] This description of the role of the person in society provided the basis for a political vocation for each member of society. Each person, endowed with a complex of human rights, was called to exercise those rights in the service of the common good and as a means of achieving his or her own full human development. This conception of citizenship is found in *Pacem in terris* and provides the basis in turn of relating person, state, and society in *Dignitatis humanae*.[11]

The idea of citizenship, therefore, is closely linked with the doctrinal development leading to *Dignitatis humanae*. Even as the Church has developed its concept of Christian as citizen, however, the role of citizenship in modern industrial societies like our own has become more complex and more difficult to sustain. The relevance of the Christian concept of citizenship is clarified today by the very problematical nature of the topic in the wider society. Professor Michael Walzer of Harvard provides a sense of the contemporary dilemma in an essay entitled "The Problem of Citizenship."[12] Walzer first considers extreme cases where citizenship becomes a problem; these include times of civil war or foreign occupation. Then he comes to the case that is closer to home in the following passage:

> But there is another case, nearer our own, where the state has simply outgrown the human reach and understanding of its citizens. It is not necessarily monstrous, divided, or subjugated, but its citizens are alienated and powerless. They experience a kind of moral uneasiness; their citizenship is a source of anxiety as well as of security and pride, and if they are not traitors in the specific sense of that word, they are sometimes hard put to explain what holds them fast.[13]

Walzer argues that the problem of citizenship today is rooted in both the conditions of the modern state and the received notions of citizenship that are available in the Western political tradition. Specifically, he contrasts the Liberal and the Aristotelian notions of citizenship, finding neither of them adequate to fit the needs of the modern state. The Liberal concept of citizenship depicts the person as purely a passive recipient of benefits from the state; there is no public participation, only private pleasure, involved in the Liberal idea of the citizen. The Liberal concept eviscerates any political or moral content from citizenship; for this reason it is unsatisfactory.

In contrast, the Aristotelian notion is a highly activist idea of citizenship. The citizen is "a man who rules and is ruled in turn."[14] The dominant motif here is active, meaningful participation in shaping the political system that frames our lives. The difficulty with this concept of citizenship is not its content but its implementation. The conditions of large bureaucratic industrial states present formidable obstacles to realizing the Aristotelian ideal. In Walzer's words, "In no state called democratic do the citizens actually exercise power; nor does that seem a lively possibility."[15] Yet some analogous form of the Aristotelian notion *should* be realized: both a sense of human dignity and sensitivity to the democratic tradition call for us to find a way for citizens to rule as well as be ruled.

Walzer's proposal for finding a way out of the contemporary dilemma holds interest for those who know the Catholic tradition. He really invokes a version of the subsidiarity principle. The way to reshape the Aristotelian ideal for contemporary conditions is in terms of the theory of democratic pluralism—a favorite theme of John Courtney Murray. A pluralist theory of democracy posits several autonomous groups or voluntary associations intervening between the citizen and state. While the citizen in isolation simply cannot influence or affect the centralized power of the state, citizens participating in intermediary groups exercise a different power in society. These groups, ranging from unions to professional associations to churches, provide the experience of the Aristotelian idea and also the channel through which the citizen approaches the state. Walzer puts the case this way: "This is surely the great strength of a pluralist citizenship: that it not only implicates the citizens in state policy, but generates real obligations and an authentic patriotism by recognizing a sphere within which they actually have scope for meaningful action."[16]

The role for the Church in this process follows from the fact that pluralist citizenship means multiple loyalties for the citizen. As citizen, the person has a relationship of loyalty and obligation to the state. But this is never absolute loyalty or an exclusive obligation. For pluralist citizenship to exist, there must be other loyalties, other obligations, that serve to test and measure the claims of the state on the citizen. In the Catholic tradition the unique countervailing loyalty to any pretensions of an absolutist state has been the transcendent relationship of the citizen with God, mediated by the institution of the Church.

Gaudium et spes, in defining the role of the Church in society, states that the Church "is at the same time the sign and safeguard of the transcendence of the human person."[17] Murray describes this sentence as the one which best summarizes the relationship of Church and society in the teaching of Vatican II. The Church protects the transcendence of the person by providing people independent ground upon which to stand in assessing the claims made upon them by the state.

The central point here is that citizens must be educated for pluralist citizenship. To maintain multiple loyalties, to measure the claims of state power, to discern means of keeping the political and economic order accountable to citizens takes a degree of public awareness and moral discernment which must be cultivated. In moral-religious terms, this cultivation of the citizenry is known as forming personal and public conscience.

Dignitatis humanae elaborated a theory of state and society which calls for a pluralist citizenship within differing social systems. *Octogesima adveniens* of Paul VI supplies a conception of the Church's role in society which complements *Dignitatis humanae*. In his call to Christians to take political responsibility seriously as part of their vocation,[18] the Pope set the groundwork for ministry in the Church that would assist people to take his call seriously. The task is pluralist in form and intention; it is not to mold Christians into a single party but to call Christians to accept diverse forms of participation in shaping society according to the norms of justice, love, truth, and freedom. To do this requires not only a pervasive sense of political responsibility among Christians, but also a precise sense of moral discernment in particular areas of life. With that in mind, I would like to exemplify the demands of multiple citizenship with two cases arising from contemporary American society.

CASES OF CONSCIENCE AND CITIZENSHIP

Freedom of religion as it is found in the Declaration of Vatican II is one of several human rights which each person possesses in virtue of his/her human dignity. The right is unique in the sense that its object is the person's transcendent relationship with God; but the exercise of the right takes place in relationship to other human and civil rights to which it is joined. When we consider the unfinished agenda of religious liberty in terms of the Church-and-society question, the relationship of religious freedom to other rights becomes clear. Two relevant examples which I intend only to describe, not to probe, are the following.

Citizenship, Conscience, and Contemporary Warfare

Gaudium et spes called for Christians "to undertake an evaluation of war with an entirely new attitude."[19] The implications of doing this in a nuclear age are profound. The issue of war is the "limit case" that tests the multiplicity of loyalties inherent in citizenship. The call to arms is seen in the secular arena as the test case of citizenship; it is the moment when the burden of citizenship falls most directly and forcefully on a person's shoulders. It is the state which has the right to call people to arms; but the decision to obey is not a purely political or secular issue. In Christian terms, the use of force is also a "limit case" in a moral sense. Hence, at the moment of the call to arms, the two deepest loyalties of the Christian citizen raise the sharpest questions. The moral-religious decision is not contained simply in "to fight or not"; it follows the one who answers the call into the complex moral dilemmas of war itself; it follows the one who resists the call throughout his way of conscientious witness.

For Christians living in the United States, the stakes and the substance of the limit case of war should be made clear. The issue remains for us a continuing pastoral question; the cultivation of an entirely new attitude to war must go on in peacetime. When the shooting starts, the climate for reasoned moral discourse diminishes. At the root of the Christian's right to evaluate the call to arms or to resist an unjustified command while in arms is the right to religious liberty, his duty to obey a higher call than the voice of the secular state. In the complexity of modern warfare the exercise of this right requires prior training.

In some sense a person's conscience must be schooled in the discipline of Christian choice.

In a nuclear armed nation the stakes of the choice can be very high indeed. The onset of nuclear weapons has fractured the centuries-old distinction between just war and pacifism in Christian tradition by creating the category of nuclear pacifism. These labels simply highlight the nature of the moral dilemma posed by contemporary warfare. Nonnuclear dimensions of the moral dilemma have been graphically illustrated in the last decade by the case of Vietnam. The exercise of religious liberty in this arena calls for a cultivated Christian conscience. This in turn places significant demands on Christian thought, education, and pastoral practice—all in the name of religious liberty.

Citizenship and the Spectrum of Rights

A second area of consideration is suggested by the concept of human rights implied in *Dignitatis humanae*. In line with the thought of *Pacem in terris*, *Dignitatis humanae* presupposes an integrated spectrum of rights rooted in the nature of the human person and spanning the areas from political and civil rights through socioeconomic rights to cultural rights. The scope of this spectrum provides a test of how we understand the concept of human rights in our own political system and in the extension of that system through the premises and practice of American foreign policy.

On the one hand, the political and civil tradition of American democracy was used as an example by Murray of how the concept of a limited state and the practice of religious freedom could be squared with Catholic teaching. In this sense we should be very much at home with *Dignitatis humanae*. On the other hand, the Declaration's concept of an integrated spectrum of human rights calls into question our tendency to distinguish sharply political and civil rights from socioeconomic privileges or rewards. The questions of which rights are necessary for a person to live in human dignity, and how those rights ought to be met, remain part of the unfinished agenda for the American political system in dealing with national economic policy and the international economic order.

In this question again the task is one of grasping the vision of the theory of society and state implied by *Dignitatis humanae* and relating it to both pastoral practice and policy guidance in the Church. Pavan's conception of society is still ahead of us; his presentation reminds us how far we have yet to go.

This thought brings me to my final comment. Ten years after Vatican II, as we face the unfinished agenda of *Dignitatis humanae* or *Gaudium et spes* or *Lumen gentium*, indeed as we face the continuing agenda of the postconciliar era in the Church, one of our great needs is a new generation of Murrays and Pavans. The Church cannot live without intellectual effort. When it declines, her light in the world diminishes.

The Council was produced in great part by a generation of outstanding theologians who labored patiently and painstakingly during the earlier part of this century and saw their work climaxed by Vatican II. Their names read like a litany: Congar, de Lubac, Chenu, Rahner, Philips, Leclercq, Häring, Diekmann, McManus, Butler, Higgins, Ahern, McKenzie, and many others. The postconciliar period needs a similar generation of thinkers, people of Christian wisdom with a sense of the Church and a sensitivity to the world. My hope is that the Woodstock Theological Center, drawing inspiration from people like Pietro Pavan and John Courtney Murray, can be an instrument for cultivating such a generation of theologians in the Church of the United States.

NOTES

[1] J. C. Murray, "The Declaration on Religious Freedom," in J. Miller, Ed., *Vatican II: An Interfaith Appraisal* (New York: Association Press, 1966) p. 565.

[2] J. C. Murray, "The Issue of Church and State at Vatican Council II," *Theological Studies* 27 (1966) 580-606.

[3] *Ibid.*, pp. 586, 590-91.

[4] Murray, "The Declaration on Religious Freedom," p. 568; also Murray, "The Problem of Religious Freedom," *Theological Studies* 25 (1964) 522.

[5]Murray, "The Problem of Religious Freedom," p. 518.

[6]Murray, "The Issue of Church and State at Vatican Council II," p. 601.

[7]*Ibid.*, pp. 599-600.

[8]Third International Synod of Bishops, *Justice in the World* (Washington, D.C.: NCCB, 1971).

[9]J. C. Murray, "Leo XIII on Church and State: The General Structure of the Controversy," *Theological Studies* 14 (1953) 1-30; "Leo XIII: Two Concepts of Government," *ibid.* 14 (1953) 551-67; "Leo XIII: Two Concepts of Government II," *ibid.* 15 (1954) 1-33; "Leo XIII: Separation of Church and State," *ibid.* 14 (1953) 145-214.

[10]Pius XII, Radio Broadcast, Christmas Eve (*AAS* 37 [1945] 12).

[11]J. C. Murray, "Key Themes in the Encyclical, *Pacem in terris*" (America Press edition, 1963) pp. 57-64.

[12]M. Walzer, *Obligations: Essays on Disobedience, War, and Citizenship* (Cambridge: Harvard Univ. Press, 1970) pp. 203-28.

[13]*Ibid.*, p. 204.

[14]*Ibid.*, p. 211.

[15]*Ibid.*, p. 216.

[16]*Ibid.*, pp. 219-20.

[17]*Gaudium et spes*, no. 76.

[18]Paul VI, *Octogesima adveniens*, no. 46 (Washington, D.C.: USCC, 1971).

[19]*Gaudium et spes*, no. 80.

Critical Reflections

George Lindbeck

The last point Monsignor Pavan emphasized, namely, the irreversibility of the Declaration on Religious Freedom, is one which Protestants devoutly hope is true. Most of us remember the preconciliar situation in which ecumenical discussions revolved around the issue of religious liberty. Non-Catholics, perhaps especially in America, were obsessed with the question of what would happen to civil and religious liberties if Catholics became a majority. They constantly asked if the Church approved of the disabilities under which non-Catholics suffered in places like Spain. This was the end-all and the be-all of most interchurch exchanges. Ecumenism could not advance under these circumstances. It was only because of the Declaration on Religious Freedom, as Monsignor Pavan says, that the way was opened for the Decree on Ecumenism. Thus any suggestion that there is something reversible about the Declaration would be extremely shocking, indeed traumatic, for Protestant sensibilities. This is paradoxical. By and large Protestants resist the notion that there is anything irreversible or infallible in the pronouncements of the Church—except in the case of this Declaration.

This does not mean, however, that Protestant enthusiasm for the Declaration is unrestricted. To be sure, Protestants by and large approve of what it says regarding the "subject" of the right to religious liberty, i.e., the universality of both its active and passive subjects. They further approve of the content of the Declaration, that is, immunity from coercion in matters religious. In reference to the foundations and the nature of this right, however, they have difficulties.

These problems have been articulated by many contemporary representatives of the Reformation tradition, and not least by Reinhold Niebuhr, who in many ways was the Protestant counterpart of John Courtney Murray on the American scene. He, like many other Protestants, was skeptical of the notion that the right to religious liberty can be grounded in an ontological human dignity that is knowable apart from revelation. Human beings are far too sinful, far too completely fallen, to be able by their own power to have or to know this ontologically-grounded human dignity. Revelation is indispensable. Without it, human reason inevitably produces contradictory and corrupt ideas of what is truly human. It is only through the Christian story, through the biblical narrative as summed up and climaxing in Jesus Christ, that the genuine nature of human dignity can be discerned.

In an odd kind of way, therefore, the Protestant tends to make not human dignity but human sinfulness the foundation of religious liberty. Sinfulness extends to all human authorities, whether civil or religious, revolutionary or conservative, Christian or non-Christian. None can be trusted in matters of conscience. Their authority must be limited precisely because they also are fallen. Democracy (of the limited rather than majoritarian and "totalitarian" kind) is *necessary*, Reinhold Niebuhr used to say, because of the human propensity for injustice (although, to be sure, it is *possible*, as he also recognized, only because of the human propensity for justice).

The Reformation tradition stresses, however, not only human evil, but also the *theologia crucis*, the theology of the cross. This in its contemporary interpretations provides a positive revelational ground for religious liberty. The cross defines what is consonant with human dignity. The methods the Church uses cannot go against the gospel, and the gospel is the gospel of the Crucified One. What Christians believe is the absolute truth comes to them through one who died selflessly that others might live; and they, as servants of the one who died that others might live, must also be willing to suffer and serve without any suggestion whatsoever of imposing their views or their positions in a coercive way upon others. This kind of argument for religious liberty is not absent from the Declaration, but it takes second place, while for much Protestant theology it is the chief or sole argument.

Now the question this raises is that of the significance of

these disagreements regarding the foundations of religious liberty. What are the policy implications, if any, of legitimating, explaining, and supporting religious liberty by reasons that are rather different from those present in the Declaration? Two possibilities occur to me here. First, the particular Protestant grounding for religious liberty that I have mentioned would seem both theoretically and de facto to give greater room for freedom within the Church: the suspicion of human authority applies also to Church authority. The other policy implication is that Protestants perhaps do not have as good a basis as Catholics for insisting that non-Christians grant religious liberty to all. Arguments from specifically Christian convictions regarding human sinfulness and the *theologia crucis* cannot claim to be as widely persuasive as those derived from an "ontological dignity" that is said to be in principle knowable apart from revelation.

These differences are not unimportant, but they need not imperil the fundamental agreement on religious liberty which now at long last, by God's grace, unites Catholics and Protestants. Without this agreement, our hopes for a more ecumenical future would be frustrate. Let us, then, hope and pray that it be a permanent, an irreversible, development in the Church's understanding of Christian truth.

Manfred H. Vogel

Monsignor Pavan and Bishop Rausch deserve our thanks and admiration for having given us two excellent and intriguing papers dealing with the issues presented in the document *Dignitatis humanae*. They have given us a forceful and yet a balanced treatment of complicated, difficult, and sensitive issues. But the spirit of this symposium and indeed of these papers is to stimulate further deliberation and examination of the issues to which *Dignitatis humanae* addresses itself. It is in this spirit that I would like to join the discussion with a few observations.

There are two central issues on the agenda here: the relationship between state and Church and the question of mission to the world. I think it is fair to say that the papers of Pavan and Rausch took what might be described as a progressive, liberal stance with regard to these issues. At the risk of exaggerating their position, I would say that I perceived the thrust of their comments as moving toward the separation of state and Church and the strong mitigation of the vocation of mission to the world. Now there is no denying that such a stance is very congenial to our *Zeitgeist*. This is an important achievement; for after all, an essential aspect of the theological enterprise is to reconcile faith with the temper of the times. In this respect the document as interpreted in the two papers makes an important step towards fulfilling this theological task.

The task of theology, however, is not only to interpret the religious teachings in a way congenial to the temper of the times but to do so in a way that at the same time will remain authentic to what we perceive to be the essential structure of the faith, and secondly in a way that will take seriously and will attempt as much as possible to conform to the tradition of the religious community. (By "tradition" here I mean the ways in which the essential structure of faith was interpreted and understood in the past.) Namely, our theologizing is circumscribed inextricably by what we perceive to be the essential structure of the faith. We cannot gain conformity with the *Zeitgeist* at the expense of the essential structure of the faith. This is a sine qua non for theologizing. Moreover, we do not start our theologizing *de novo*. We theologize in the context of a tradition, in the context of past interpretations and perceptions of what the essential structure of the faith is. And while our theologizing is not shackled to the tradition in the way it is to the essential structure of faith, it certainly bears a responsibility to the tradition that every effort be made to come to terms with it.

Of course, Pavan and Rausch have clearly shown that they are fully cognizant of these requirements and indeed have tried to satisfy them. But the question remains whether they have succeeded. Prima facie, it would seem to me that the position presented (and this applies especially to Pavan, even though he devoted a great deal of his paper to examining the tradition and joining the argument with the more conservative position) deviates from the position that the Church has held traditionally in the past with regard to these issues, i.e., with regard to the issue of the Church-state relationship and to the issue of mission to the world. According to my understanding, the traditional position of the Church was to see an intimate relationship between the state and the Church and to see the mission to the world as a central and essential ingredient in the vocation of the Church. The position regarding the relationship between state and Church presented by Pavan struck me as being protestantic (although Pavan based his position on the argument of the "ontological dignity" of man, an argument that would seem to imply the rejection of the view that man is in a fallen state—a position that may well be congenial to Judaism but not, I suspect, to Protestantism). But these problems, whether the position is in consonance with the essential structure of the faith and whether it can come to terms with the tradition, are problems within the sphere of Christian theology, and I, not being a Christian theologian, must therefore leave them to my colleagues who are Christian theologians.

I can only respond to the positions put forth by Monsignor Pavan and Bishop Rausch from the outside, more specifically from the Jewish side (though, while Judaism is certainly outside the sphere of Christianity, there is nonetheless a dimension in which both Judaism and Christianity are lodged in one and the same sphere, this being the sphere of Hebrew Scripture: to the extent that both Judaism and Christianity see themselves as the continued expression of Hebrew Scripture, of biblical faith, the two are ultimately lodged in one and the same sphere, thus mitigating the externality of one to the other). This being the case, I must hasten to warn you that with regard to these questions of the relationship between state and Church and mission to the world (as indeed with regard to practically every other question) there are different views within Judaism. As you know, if you have two Jews you get three opinions. Thus, it should be understood that I am speaking here as an individual and in no way claiming to represent Jewry or any segment of it. Even more seriously, the variety is not only subjective in terms of the way Jews perceive their heritage but is objectively lodged within the phenomenon of Judaism itself. Namely, Judaism and indeed also Christianity are, as historical entities, compounded of a variety of distinct and different structures of faith which are held together by virtue of a sharing in a common system of symbols and rituals. (In the case of Judaism, the most important "cement" is the added factor of a common belongingness to the ethnic peoplehood of Israel.) To say, therefore, that one is speaking from the vantage point of Judaism is ambiguous. Since the vantage point is determined by the structure of faith, there can be a number of vantage points all legitimately claiming to be Jewish. My remarks, therefore, will reflect only one kind of a Jewish response, without excluding the possibility of there being other kinds of Jewish response to these questions. However, I would want to argue that the vantage point from which I speak is grounded in an important and central structure of faith of historical Judaism, a structure of faith that is most intimately linked to the prophetic biblical structure of faith. In addition, this vantage point has the advantage of presenting an alternative approach to these questions, thus allowing us to examine the positions presented by Pavan and Rausch more thoroughly and profoundly. To fully delve into the significance and implications of a thesis, one should confront it with an antithesis.

Before plunging into my analysis, however, it is only fair to admit that in all probability the vast majority of emancipated Jewry today would greatly welcome this reformulation of the position of the Church with regard to the question of the relationship between state and Church (still it should be noted that the position of orthodox Jewry in diaspora may be less clear-cut and that judging by its practice in the state of Israel it would reject our notion of the separation of state and Church); and as regards the question of mission, the totality of Jewry, both orthodox and nonorthodox, would greatly welcome the reformulation expressed by Pavan and Rausch. But it would seem to me that this reaction of contemporary Jewry does not issue from religious-theological considerations; namely, its reaction is not because it perceives the essential structure of its faith to require it. Rather, its reaction in these instances is determined by psychological and prudential considerations. This is fully understandable. Let us face it: the Jews in the past have paid a high price in suffering because the state was a Christian state and because the Church pursued a policy of missionizing. The Jew feels a threat to his survival in the missionizing activity of the Church and a curtailment of his civil liberties in a state intimately linked to the Church. But as I said above, I am not concerned here with the stance that contemporary Jewry may take but rather with the stance that an essential structure of faith of Judaism would dictate with regard to these questions. And here the situation is quite different.

Indeed, an authentic dialogue between Judaism and Christianity can be carried out only in terms of the essential structures of faith manifested by the two communities. We must allow each community of faith to express its essential structure of faith fully and freely. We cannot allow political, psychological, prudential, or any other considerations to place constraints on the expression of the essential structure of faith. An encounter on the basis of political, social, or economic considerations is a bargaining conference but not an authentic dialogue. This is not to say that such an encounter is not legitimate, only that it is not legitimate as an authentic dialogue. In a different context, on a different level, such encounter may well be quite legitimate. Here, however, we are attempting to engage in authentic dialogue.

Indeed, in the context of a Jewish-Christian dialogue the two issues under discussion today, namely, the relationship of state to Church and the question of mission to the world, are significant and timely. The issue of mission to the world goes to the very heart of the relationship between Judaism and Christianity; for if one is to accept both Judaism and Christianity as authentic enterprises within the divine economy of redemption (namely, if Christianity is not to reject Judaism as superfluous and dead and if Judaism is not to reject Christianity as false and corrupted), then one is inevitably called upon to provide a rationale and a justification for the presence of both within the divine economy of redemption, and the question of mission to the world may well provide this rationale by introducing a "division of labor" between the two communities of faith. Likewise, the issue of the relationship between state and Church is of central significance in the contemporary situation in which Judaism and Christianity find themselves. For what we see today is a Christianity that has wielded power since the days of Constantine losing this power and thus, in a sense, being driven into exile-existence. At the same time, we see a Judaism that during the same period is forced to exist in exile, devoid of power, regaining a measure of power by its reentry into profane history with the reestablishment of the State of Israel in 1948 (the fact that the power placed at its disposal is minimal is not important; the quantitative aspect of more or less power is not essential to the consideration here). Thus, in authentic dialogue Christianity may learn something from the experience of Judaism in adapting to exile-existence, while Judaism can learn a great deal from Christianity about the problematics and dangers that inevitably accompany the wielding of power. Thus an ongoing discussion and exploration of these two issues should prove highly beneficial both to Christianity and to Judaism. Toward this end my following brief observations are addressed.

Let me first address myself to the question of mission. Judaism is generally portrayed as a nonmissionizing religion, and there is some truth in this claim. Certainly, judging by the stance toward missionizing that Judaism has adopted throughout most of its diaspora existence, it was not a missionizing religion in the same way that Christianity or Islam were. Indeed, not only was Judaism not pursuing an active missionizing policy, but for the most part it actively discouraged and rejected prospective converts. It is not true, however, to claim that Judaism never missionized. It is important to note that there were instances in Jewish history in which Judaism actively pursued a policy of missionizing, for this shows that Judaism is capable of pursuing a missionizing policy. Indeed, a case can be made that it is precisely in these instances where Judaism pursued a missionizing policy that its essential structure of faith was most fully and adequately expressed. Grounded in biblical monotheism, the essential structure of faith of Judaism should require that its vocation be universally applicable, and this, in turn, implicates the pursuance of missionizing. Thus, according to this rationale it is precisely in those instances when Judaism pursued an active policy of missionizing that it expressed most authentically its essential structure of faith. The nonmissionizing stance adopted by Judaism for so many centuries was dictated not by its essential structure of faith but by contingent historical circumstances that truncated and hampered the full, authentic expression of its essential structure of faith, as, for example, the all-absorbing preoccupation of Judaism with its own survival in diaspora, the dangers and difficulties that masses of new converts may pose to such survival, the prohibition of missionizing imposed on Judaism from the outside, etc. But by the same token we would have to admit that in Christianity, to the extent that it too grounds itself in biblical monotheism, the essential structure of faith would likewise require universal applicability of its vocation, which, in turn, would dictate the pursuit of mission to the world. In Christianity, however, since it was not hampered by the problematic of diaspora-existence, this requirement for universality and mission to the world could be fully and forcefully expressed.

But while I would want to argue that there is some validity in this argument, I must nevertheless admit that in the last analysis it does not afford a full and satisfactory account for the nonmissionary stance of Judaism. To account for the nonmissionary stance of Judaism purely in terms of the contingent historical circumstances of its diaspora-existence is not satisfactory. The nonmissionary stance is deeply embedded within Judaism and seems to flow from the inner depth of its life. It does not seem to be a mere superficial and external accommodation to the pressures of external reality; it seems to flow from the inner reality of Jewish life and as such from the very structure of its faith. But if this is the case, then the question immediately arises as to how Judaism can reconcile this stance with its grounding in biblical monotheism. The answer is that it does it by deferring the universal applicability of its monotheistic vocation to the eschaton, i.e., to that point in the future when its task will have been fulfilled and its vocation realized. For the time being, until the messianic era is ushered in, it leaves the world to itself, concentrating its attention on the Jewish people exclusively. In other words, while the fulfillment of its monotheistic vocation is in terms of the world at large, the redemptive work of bringing about this fulfillment is confined to the Jewish people. The world is excluded from the redemptive task (hence the nonmissionary stance of Judaism) but not from its fulfillment (hence the safeguarding of the monotheistic vocation). In this way the nonmissionizing stance of Judaism is determined not only by contingent historical circumstances but by the very structure of its faith. We should note, however, that although by this formulation Judaism is by its very structure nonmissionary, it is not at the same time also parochial. It is saved from parochialism precisely by the fact that its task when fulfilled is universally applicable. As such, even for the time being, when the redemptive task is confined to the Jewish people, the task is not of a parochial nature but infused with universal significance: it is carried, in the last analysis, not for the sake of the Jewish people alone but for the sake of mankind.

Still, it must be admitted that this stance of Judaism, though innerly consistent, may well prove unsatisfactory to many people. Thus, it is left unclear how the redemptive task which is confined to one people is transferred when fulfilled to the world at large. Linked to this, but even more problematic, is the fact that the world at large, while given to enjoy the fruits of the redemptive task when fulfilled, is excluded from participating in the task itself (members of the world at large can participate in the labor of the task only by joining the Jewish peoplehood). Why should the task be confined to one nation and not to all nations? Furthermore, and perhaps most problematically, how can the nations of the world avail themselves of the truth when they are not made cognizant of it? I, for one, would have to admit that at this point the formulation of Judaism is not complete nor is it really satisfactory. It is precisely at this juncture, therefore, that a case can be made whereby from the Jewish point of view a function can be allocated to Christianity within the economy of redemption: Christianity can enter the picture and be justified as the missionary agent of monotheistic biblical faith. The incorporation of mankind within the very work of redemption, an aspect on which Judaism is unclear and neglectful, can thus be safeguarded by Christianity. This means, however, that according to the logic of this case not only can Judaism acquiesce in the Christian vocation of mission to the world, but it indeed must require it. However, by the very same logic Judaism would have to insist that Jews be excluded from being an object for the Christian vocation of mission, since, as Rosenzweig has said, Jews are already with the Father.

I am certainly sticking my neck out in making a case for the Christian vocation of mission to the world. The very notion of mission is anathema to our *Zeitgeist*; and specifically within the Jewish community the Christian vocation of mission arouses, and with very good reason, a bad taste and ominous feelings. Still, some seminal Jewish thinkers, as for example Maimonides and Rosenzweig, did uphold the Christian vocation of mission to the world, and they did it precisely in consequence of their understanding of the vocation of Judaism and the role allotted to it in the divine economy of redemption. Of course, in the last analysis, it is up to the Christian theologian to decide whether or not his Christian vocation of faith demands of him the task of missionizing to the world. If the answer is in the affirmative, then first of all, I as his opposite partner in dialogue cannot for the sake of authentic dialogue prohibit him from so confessing his vocation; in authentic dialogue each partner should express his position fully, openly, and freely—ulterior considerations are not permissible nor can any conditions or restrictions be imposed a priori. But furthermore, I as the Jewish opposite partner to the dialogue may well accept such a confession of faith with empathy and sympathy. Empathy because being grounded, as a Jew, in the same monotheistic biblical faith I can understand the demand that flows from it for universal concern. Let us face it: monotheistic biblical faith is universal, absolute, and exclusive in its claim. We may not compromise this for the sake of being popular with the *Zeitgeist*. Oh, I do not think that it is ethically right not to be concerned with one's fellow man, nor do I think that it is religiously authentic (at least in the context of biblical faith) to give up the absolute and exclusive nature of the claim placed upon us. Sympathy because I as a Jew may see the Christian mission to the world as a completion of the redemptive task placed upon me by monotheistic biblical faith. Thus a case can be made that while Jews today, for historical and psychological reasons, would certainly want to see Christianity give up its mission to the world, Judaism in terms of its essential structure of faith as a monotheistic biblical faith would not.

But having come forth so strongly in the defense of Christian mission to the world, it is imperative that I make crystal clear that the same logic that demands the task of missionizing to the world, i.e., the logic of monotheistic biblical faith, also demands the total renunciation of the use of coercion in any form, shape, or manner in the execution of the task. By the same token that the essential structure of biblical faith, in contradistinction to that of paganism, places a claim that is universal and exclusive, it also, and here too in contradistinction to the structure of paganism, excludes the resort to coercion. Paganism may not place a universal and exclusive claim; it may be, so to speak, tolerant; but it also does not exclude coercion— the use of coercion in its adoption does not invalidate the adoption. As against this, with monotheistic biblical faith the use of coercion in its adoption should, strictly speaking, ipso facto invalidate the adoption; its adoption can be valid and authentic only when it is effected by the free will and decision of the individual. In biblical faith the relation between man and God is an I-Thou relation, and an I-Thou relation cannot be based on coercion; in paganism, on the other hand, the relation is an I-It relation which in its very nature implicates coercion. Thus the slightest manifestation of coercion would at once corrupt biblical faith and reduce it to a form of paganism. (By the way, here, in the fact that man in his relation to God is a Thou, lies the source of the "ontological dignity" ascribed to man, a consideration which played such a central role in Monsignor Pavan's paper. Only a Thou can be invested with "ontological dignity"; in the last analysis, an It can never be the carrier of "ontological dignity.")

Furthermore, aside from the fact that biblical faith and co-ercion are mutually exclusive, there is another consideration operative in biblical faith (but not in paganism) which would forbid resort to coercion. The very same fact that compels bibli-cal faith to claim exclusiveness, universalism, and absoluteness for its truth, namely, the fact that its God is the only God uni-versal and absolute, forbids biblical man to confuse himself with his God. Biblical man is not and can never be divine; he is finite and fallible. Thus in the structure of biblical faith an absolute, exclusive, and universal truth is mediated through an agency that is finite and fallible, and this introduces an inescapable tension into the structure of biblical faith. The man of biblical faith must proclaim his truth as universal, absolute, and exclusive, yet at the same time he must be always mindful of the possibili-ty (but it is only a possibility and not an inescapable necessity) that he might have perceived it wrongly, so that what he pro-claims is not the truth but idolatry. If this is forgotten, biblical man falls into fanaticism, and fanaticism is the corruption of the very essence of biblical faith. Biblical man must walk "the narrow ridge": he must claim absoluteness but he must claim it with trepidation. Ultimate certainty and self-assuredness are not his lot. As such, resort to coercion is not admissible.

But alas, walking "the narrow ridge" is not easy and there is no denying that thus far we have all too often failed misera-bly. (I suppose it is true to say that in this respect Christianity is carrying by far the heavier burden, but this is due to the fact that for so long it has had at its disposal the power to coerce; Judaism, I dare say, is saved from a heavier burden of guilt by the fact that for so long it did not have this power at its dispos-al.) The solution, however, to this pernicious problem does not lie in giving up our concern for universality or our claim to the exclusivity and absoluteness of the truth. The solution lies in devising a way whereby the monotheistic truth can be pro-claimed without resort to coercion. I fully realize that this is easier said than done and that coercion manifests itself in a hundred and one different ways, many of them of the most in-sidious nature. Still, it is toward this end that our efforts must be directed. We may perhaps receive some guidance here from rabbinic Judaism; for rabbinic Judaism, in withdrawing from active missionizing, adopted a stance that may be taken as missionizing by example—one witnesses by example. It is the life we lead, the actions we perform, that manifest the truth to others. Here, however, the activity, the coercion if you please, is directed toward ourselves, not toward others. But in doing so we let the light shine to others. In any event, the pursuit of a way by which we can carry our witness to every person without resort to coercion is the subject that should be on the agenda, and it is a subject that can greatly profit from an authentic dialogue between Judaism and Christianity.

With regard to the second issue, the issue of the relationship between state and Church, its treatment in Jewish thought is rather limited, particularly when compared to the rich and sophisticated treatment that it receives in Christian thought. While the issue has always been an important issue in Christian thought, in Judaism it is at best peripheral. This may be due to the fact that Judaism for so much of its life existed in diaspora, where the issue could not arise. For Judaism existing in diaspora the issue was academic and purely theoretical: if you do not have a state, you do not worry about the relationship that it may or may not have with religion. But perhaps there is a deeper reason, a reason that is determined by the very structure of Judaism and not merely by the contingent circumstances of its existence, which accounts for the fact that the issue is not central in Jewish thought. Let me attempt to briefly delineate what I have in mind.

The very presence of the issue of the relationship between state and Church presupposes a division and separation between the domain of religion and the domain of the state. Only when the two domains constitute two distinct, separate, and mutually exclusive entities can the question arise whether there is a relation between the two and, if so, what kind of a relation it should be. Thus, the issue of the relationship between state and Church would arise in a context where the domain of religion is seen to refer exclusively to the relationship between man and God, i.e., to the vertical relationship and the spiritual dimension that manifest themselves in the inward life of the person, while, in contradistinction to this, the domain of the state is seen to refer to the relationship between man and man, i.e., to the horizontal relationship and the material-temporal dimension that manifest themselves in the external actions of the person. While religion refers to the relationship between man and God, the state refers to relationship between man and man; while religion refers to the vertical relation, the state refers to the horizontal relation; while religion is spiritual, the state is temporal; while religion deals with the inward life, the state deals with external action. In such a context the issue of the relationship between the two domains must inevitably arise.

Such a division between the domain of religion and the domain of the state may well characterize the structure of Christianity, and consequently we should not be surprised that the issue of the relationship between state and Church is and has always been an important issue in Christian thought. Of course, as to the precise delineation of the relationship there could be different formulations, and we do indeed find a variety of formulations within Christianity on this question. Thus, it is my impression that the traditional Catholic formulation did maintain a definite link between the two domains, indeed a link in which the domain of the state was to be subjected to the domain of the Church (though under the exigencies of the time the requirement of subjugation had to be mitigated and various other formulations evolved as a modus vivendi). On the other hand, it is my impression that in Lutheran Protestantism the thrust has been in the opposite direction, namely, toward the isolation and disassociation of the two domains. Man lives in two isolated spheres: in the spiritual sphere of vertical relation and inwardness, where the ultimate and real significance of life lies, and in the mundane sphere of horizontal relations which he is to endure for the duration; the mundane sphere is in no way involved in the drama of salvation of the individual nor does the religious sphere in any way impinge upon the mundane. But let me not get sidetracked by the many specific formulations that were developed in Christian thought (the traditional Catholic formulation and the Lutheran Protestant formulation by no means exhaust the list). The point that I want to make here is that all the formulations within the context of Christianity presuppose, in my judgment, the constitution of the religious domain as separate and distinct from the domain of the state.

In contradistinction to the position of Christianity (as I perceive it), Judaism rejects the very notion of the division between the domain of religion and the domain of the state. In Judaism the religious domain encompasses the domain of the state; the vertical relation goes through and is constituted by the horizontal relation, which, in turn, means that the horizontal relation is inextricably constituted as but a segment of the vertical relation; man relates to God through his relation to his fellow man (as such, by the way, the entity constituting the human pole in the divine-human relation is the community and not the individual, the individual participating in the relation only by virtue of his membership in the community and only through the mediation of the community); the spiritual is realized in the mundane; in short, it is in the horizontal dimension, in the domain of the state, that the religious vocation is consummated. Thus, in the context of Judaism there can be in principle no separation between the domain of religion and the domain of the state, between the spiritual and the mundane, and consequently the Church-state issue cannot authentically arise. Indeed, the religious law of Deuteronomy addresses itself to the domains of civil law, criminal law, international law, and politics just as readily and naturally as it addresses itself to the domain of rituals. The prophets are concerned with social and economic justice, with international politics, as much and as fervently as they are concerned with the worship of other gods and fetishism. And the Talmud, following in the footsteps of biblical law, encompasses in its Halacha every conceivable aspect of human life. Evidently, in such a context the issue of state and Church does not make sense.

True, today in the State of Israel we have what may be described as a state-church issue. But it would seem to me that this is due to the fact that emancipated Jewry is all too prone to perceive and understand the phenomenon of religion as it is perceived and understood in the West, i.e., according to the model of Christian understanding, and not as it is perceived and understood in Judaism. And even so, a good case can be made that the issue encountered in the State of Israel today is not really the state-church issue but rather the issue of what is the appropriate religious expression for Judaism in the new circumstances that the reestablishment of the state has created—whether orthodoxy, the religious expression of Judaism in diaspora, remains the appropriate expression also in the context of statehood or whether a new expression must evolve.

To return to my main theme, however, let me conclude by saying that Western modern cultural awareness, if it does not reject religion altogether, would like to confine the domain of religion exclusively to the vertical relation, making it the private affair of the individual's inwardness, thus excluding religion from the domain of the state, the horizontal network of relations between man and man. If it tolerates religion at all, it would tolerate it best in its Lutheran-Protestant formulation. As such, religion in accepting this confinement will, of course, greatly reduce the friction and tension with modern cultural awareness and will, no doubt, earn a good many brownie points for it. But the question is whether in doing so religion does not really commit suicide or, to change the metaphor, whether in doing so religion does not succeed in merely smoothing and gracing its own exit from the stage; for the arena of concern for modern man is overwhelmingly the horizontal domain, the concrete temporal world, the domain of the relations between man and man. The concerns of modern man are not otherworldly; they are very much this-worldly. In relegating religion, therefore, to the otherworldly sphere and excluding it from involvement in this-worldly concerns, one in effect relegates religion to irrelevancy. And a religion that is irrelevant might for all intents and purposes be dead.

It will not do for us to ignore the demands and temper of our *Zeitgeist*. We must listen to it attentively and summon all our resources to understand it in depth and in sympathy. But in doing so we must also not forget the demands and constrictions that the authentic structure of our faith places upon us. In our day, in the context of modern cultural awareness, this dual assignment is not an easy task. But I submit that this is the only authentic way that is open to us: we must come to terms with and satisfy both the demands of modern cultural awareness and the demands of the authentic structure of our faith. It is precisely because of this conviction and in view of the fact that Monsignor Pavan and Bishop Rausch have addressed themselves to the former demands, i.e., the demands of modern cultural awareness, that I have undertaken to stress the demands and considerations of the authentic structure of faith as I perceive it. I hope that in this way I succeeded in contributing a little to our deliberations. I think we can all agree that the issues confronting us are of great difficulty and complexity and that we all have a long way to go before a satisfactory solution is in sight.

Walter J. Burghardt, S.J.

In the wake of Pietro Pavan's magisterial presentation, several facets of contemporary Catholic doctrine on religious freedom leave me less than happy, leave me uneasy. My uneasiness has to do with four interrelated issues: state religion, the constitutional model of the state, development of doctrine, and irreversibility.

First, state religion. On a number of occasions John Courtney Murray made clear a conviction of his: *Dignitatis humanae* "disavows the legal institution of state religion that in various ways was characteristic of the sacral society. . . . [Legal establishment of religion is regarded as] hypothetical, as a matter of circumstances, not of doctrine. Thus . . . the notion of the sacral society is dismissed into history, beyond recall. The free society of today is recognized to be secular" (in *America*, April 23, 1966, p. 593).

This, I admit, is one thrust of the Declaration on Religious Freedom, and it seems to follow inescapably from Paul VI's address of December 8, 1965, to the world's governments: "What does the Church ask of you today? Nothing but freedom." And still I am troubled. Why? The Declaration recognizes that "peculiar circumstances" may call for "special legal recognition" in favor of a particular religious community—e.g., the Roman Catholic Church. Is it not still possible, therefore, that in a civil society that is predominantly Catholic the demands of public order may dictate that some Protestant "be restrained from acting publicly in accordance with his own beliefs"? And if such restraint is to be explained as a matter of historical circumstances, presumably regrettable, not commanded by Catholic "doctrine," should not Catholics themselves, in the light of *Dignitatis humanae*, work to make such privileges unnecessary, since they offend against "doctrine"?

This leads naturally to my second trouble area: the constitutional model of the state. If Pavan and Murray are correct, the right to religious freedom as proclaimed in *Dignitatis humanae* cannot "be harmonized with a juridical system other than that inspired by the model of the constitutional state," what Pavan calls "the democratic-social state founded on law." Why? Because this is the only form of state that of its nature is capable of recognizing and implementing the natural right of every citizen to religious freedom, the right that stems from the dignity of the human person. But does not this imply that the constitutional model is the one model of state which, unlike "Catholic states or states calling themselves Catholic," unlike any and all confessional states, is not "a product of a particular historical situation" but "called for by the gospel"? If so, does not the Declaration canonize the constitutional state, declare that where such a form of government does *not* exist, it can only be a tolerated situation, due to unfortunate circumstances which all persons of good will ought to work to alter?

If true, this would be a fascinating turnabout from the Catholic vision before 1965. Then, for all but a few insightful thinkers like Murray and Pavan, the Catholic state was the ideal, was doctrine, a secular or a democratic-social state was the contingently historical, no more than tolerable. Now, it would seem, the democratic-social state is "doctrine," the confessional state at best tolerable. But can Catholicism, in consistency with its political theology, in harmony with Paul VI's call for "nothing but freedom," set its seal definitively on one model of political government?

This leads logically to a third concern: doctrinal development. The Declaration on Religious Freedom was, as Murray saw, "the most controversial document of the whole Council, largely because it raised with sharp emphasis the issue that lay continually below the surface of all the conciliar debates—the issue of the development of doctrine" (in Walter M. Abbott, ed., *The Documents of Vatican II* [New York: America Press, 1966] p.‎ 673). In basing religious freedom on the dignity of the human person, in discarding the post-Reformation and nineteenth-century theory of civil tolerance of false religions, in claiming from the state "nothing but freedom," in dismissing into history the legal institution of state religion, in the philosophy of society and state that undergirds the document, has Vatican II done no more than discard transient, fugitive elements in the Church's tradition, or is it more faithful to history to affirm that the Church has discarded "the tradition"?

Murray was convinced that in *Dignitatis humanae* the Council was bringing forth from the treasury of truth "a doctrine that is at once new and also in harmony with traditional teaching" (*ibid.*, p. 678, n. 4). In so speaking, he was raising implicitly one of the most explosive questions in contemporary theology: how much discontinuity is compatible with Catholic continuity? Not, *is* discontinuity compatible, but how much? I submit that the question cannot be answered in the abstract. The solution lies in the Church's life: where in fact are the discontinuities, and how Catholic are they? Concretely, what is the evolution from 1832 to 1965, from Gregory XVI's *Mirari vos* to Vatican II's *Dignitatis humanae*? Is it a movement simply from obscurity to greater enlightenment, a better understanding of our genuine tradition, or must we say that, in the area of religious freedom, Catholicism now rejects what in the nineteenth century it held as "doctrine"? Here is a neuralgic issue for a doctoral candidate tearing his shaggy mane in search of a dissertation topic.

Which leads inexorably to my fourth unease: irreversibility. Is the Declaration on Religious Freedom unalterable Catholic doctrine? Pavan insists that the basic affirmation of the document is indeed irreversible. Why? Because "it is a right founded in the dignity of the human person." But what is to keep the

Church from saying "It is *not* a right founded in the dignity of the human person: this is what we thought in 1965, but times have changed"? In this connection, I am fascinated (perhaps excessively) by the adverb in Paul VI's famous question: "What does the Church ask of you [rulers and governments] *today?*" Might the Church ask for something more than freedom, a position of privilege, tomorrow? And if so, on what grounds?

Some of my tentative conclusions, on a tenuous theological limb: (1) I am convinced that Vatican II's affirmation of religious freedom as based on the dignity of the human person, though implicit in "the gospel," is discontinuous with certain explicit elements within the Catholic tradition; and I am happy that it is. (2) Even though the Declaration is not "defined" doctrine, I do not see how the Church can reverse itself on religious freedom and its foundation without coming into conflict with reason and the gospel. (3) Nevertheless, I do not believe that, in the real order in which we humans must live, we can dismiss the possibility of a confessional state—unlikely perhaps, but not impossible. (4) In such a political situation, I do not see how the "religion of the state," if it means anything, can really grant equal rights to those who do not share the faith of the vast majority. (5) Therefore I must conclude that the genuinely confessional state is not in accord with Catholic doctrine (has it, therefore, ever been?). Catholic doctrine can only *tolerate* a confessional state, even a Catholic state, as the lesser of two evils, to be corrected as soon as possible.

These reflections have as their primary purpose to suggest that a continuing task within Catholic theology will be to deepen our understanding of the Declaration's affirmations and the reasons on which they repose. It is not only statements with which we *dis*agree that theologians must appraise and reappraise. *Dignitatis humanae,* for all its thrilling truth, is not a dogmatic definition, and it will not do to replace a theological tyranny of the "right" with a tyranny of those who, as Murray said of himself, represent the "extreme center." Civilized argument, even Catholic argument, is not arrested by a Council vote of 2308 for, 70 against.

BRIEF BIOGRAPHIES

Monsignor Pietro Pavan, born 1903 in northern Italy, was ordained in 1928, studied at the Gregorian University in Rome and the University of Padua, and earned degrees in philosophy (1930), theology (1932), and economics and social sciences (1935). For a quarter century he was professor of social economics at the Lateran in Rome, from 1969 to 1974 its rector. Author of a score of books on the social order, democracy, and religious freedom, e.g., *The Catholic Laity and the Temporal Order*, Msgr. Pavan became particularly known throughout the world for the major role he played in the drafting of Pope John XXIII's encyclical *Pacem in terris*. In the preparatory phase of Vatican II he was a member of two subcommissions of the Theological Commission, dealing respectively with the apostolate of the laity and the socioeconomic order. As a Council *peritus*, he helped prepare several of the documents, including Schema 13 on the Church in the Modern World. He collaborated intimately with John Courtney Murray at every stage in the development of the Declaration on Religious Freedom. Because of his unique familiarity with this document, he was chosen to write the commentaries on it for two major international projects on the interpretation of Vatican II. He is second to none as a living authority on *Dignitatis humanae*.

Bishop James S. Rausch, born 1928 in Albany, Minnesota, studied at St. John's University in Collegeville, was ordained in 1956, did graduate work at the College of St. Thomas in St. Paul, at the University of Minnesota, and at the Gregorian University in Rome, where he received a Ph.D. degree (1969) after studies in pastoral sociology and development economics. Bishop Rausch has been active with the United States Catholic Conference since 1968. After serving several years as associate general secretary of the USCC, he was chosen in 1972 general secretary both to the USCC and the National Conference of Catholic Bishops, a double post he continues to hold. He was ordained a bishop in April 1973. Besides occupying posts of high administrative responsibility in the Church, Bishop Rausch has continued to do scholarly work. He has edited a book entitled *The Family of Nations* and has written numerous articles and delivered many addresses dealing with human rights, foreign aid, peace, and justice.

George Lindbeck, professor at the Yale Divinity School, was born in China of missionary parents and studied in north China, Hong Kong, and Korea before returning to college in the United States. He did his doctoral work at Yale University, with a dissertation on Duns Scotus. An observer at Vatican II for the Lutheran World Federation and extraordinarily active in ecumenical dialogues since that time, he has authored a number of books, including *The Future of Roman Catholicism*.

Manfred Vogel, professor in the Department of Religious Studies at Northwestern University, was born in Tel Aviv and came to the United States at seventeen. He received rabbinic ordination after studies at the Jewish Theological Seminary in New York, and holds a Ph.D. in philosophy from Columbia University. Before coming to Northwestern, he taught philosophy at Brandeis and served as chaplain there. He has written extensively on Feuerbach, Buber, and others.

Walter J. Burghardt, S.J., professor of patristic theology at the Catholic University of America, has his doctorate in theology from that institution, and taught for twenty-eight years at the Jesuit school of theology, Woodstock College. He is editor in chief of the quarterly *Theological Studies* and research associate at the Woodstock Theological Center. Author of five books, he has written over a hundred articles for various journals.